LEAN & AGILE

Project Management

T0103847

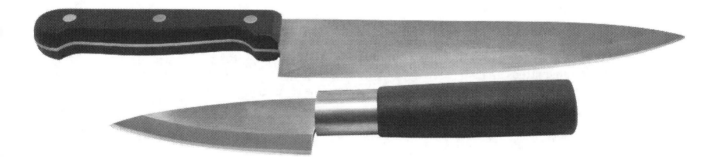

pablolledó
projectManagement

Bibliographic cataloging information:
Paul Leido
Lean & Agile: Project Management
1st ed. – United States: the author, 2014.
147 p. ; 28x22 cm.

1. Administration. 2. Management.

Editor: Luis Santana, PMP®, CBCP, CISA

Pictures and Images:
    Cover Art © Samanta Gallego
    Images © Paul Leido
    Screens © @Risk in Appendix A
    Screens © MS Project in Appendix A

Appendix B: Cecilia Boggi
Appendix C: Esteban Zuttion
Translation: Luis Santana

For: Marcela, Maximo, Martin, and Salvador

Contents

PART III – THE 10 COMMANDMENTS

PART IV — APPENDICES

ABOUT THE AUTHOR

Paul Leido. Master of Science in Project Analysis, Finance and Investments, University of York. PMP®, Project Management Institute. MBA in Project Management, Francisco de Vitoria University. MBA in International Business, Universitat de Lleida. Bachelor in Economics, Cuyo University. Founder and actual President of four enterprises. Distinguished International Professor in Project Management. Author of 8 Project Management books.

Training and Consulting offered in more than 20 countries, to more than 15,000 executives of international companies. PMI Distinguished Contribution Award.

If you have legally acquired this book, you can contact me with any questions or comments at: pl@pablolledo.com

ABOUT THE EDITOR

Luis Santana. PMP, Certified Business Continuity Professional (CBCP) and Certified Information Systems Auditor (CISA). Bachelor in Management of Information Systems. Co-founder and President of Business Essentials, Inc. He has more than 15 years of experience as a Project Manager and has practiced the profession in both private and public sectors in the USA. Luis stands out as one of the best CBCPs in his Region and is considered an expert on the field.

If you got this PDF book without buying it, you can buy it at www.pablolledo.com for USD 8,90, in order to contribute to your professional ethics.

*10% of the sales from this book are donated to **CONIN**, a non-for-profit organization, created by Doctor Abel Albino, who fights against childhood undernourishment.*

PROLOGUE

My former student, Paul Leido, is undoubtedly one of the younger authors with the greatest projection in the industry of project and one whom I consider a colleague and friend.

We are always surprised by his inexhaustible capacity to investigate and publish new and interesting material with every one of his books.

This book proposes lean-agile project management as a way to improve efficiency in project management. The book focuses on the following two basic concepts: value and waste. Maximizing the former is as important as minimizing the latter.

He guides us with clear explanations, multiple examples, and illustrative graphics in every well-organized chapter. Most importantly, he presents many interesting cases and stories to clarify every concept about agile project management.

Unlike other books about project management that delve into the development of PERT, flowcharts, Gantt charts, etc. (like one of my books), this is an easy to read book that provides effective and useful tools. It also helps the readers with its original "Lessons Learned" at the end of each chapter, which differs from the typical "Chapter Summary" that generally does not add any value.

Anybody who wants to specialize in project management or any of its phases, not only needs to read this book, but use it as a permanent source of information.

Nassir Sapag Chain
Engineer at the University of Chile
Author of more than 20 books about Project Analysis

PART **I**

LEAN & AGILE PHILOSOPHIES

1   INTRODUCTION

A start never disappears, not even with an ending.

HARRY MULISCH (1927-2010)
Dutch novelist

Before starting, we would like to make it clear that this book has its origins from the thoughts of great Authors and books like:

- James P. Womack, Daniel T. Jones, and Daniel Roos (Author), "**The Machine that changes the world**"
- Ronald Mascitelli, "**Building a Project Driven Enterprise**"

After reading those international bestsellers aligned to Lean principles, we decide to write a book that includes Agile concepts as well.

This book "Lean and Agile Project Management" is a special edition of our previous book "Lean Project Management" published by Pearson Prentice Hall in 2006.

We hope you enjoy reading the book, as much as we enjoy writing it.

Throughout the book we will see many case studies, all of them real, but changing names and places in order to protect the confidentiality of those involved.

The main **capabilities** that you will get when you finish this book are:

1. **Accelerate** projects…, without adding costs and reducing quality.
2. Achieve **efficiencies** in project management, by eliminating waste.

To achieve these objectives of "speed" and "efficiency" in project management, the topics that we will cover throughout the book are:

- Project success and failures
- Evolution of **good practices**
- Types of **times**
- **Lean** thinking
- The **Agile** Manifesto
- Time **Batches**
- Transaction **costs**
- 10 tips for an **Agile Leader**

1.1   SUCCESSFUL PROJECT

Both failure and success are relative. It all depends on the definition or the standard that we may want to use to measure a project.

Even though project management techniques have been used since many centuries ago, the peak and development of specific tools began to deepen starting in 1960.

In the **1960s**, the success of a project was defined based on its **quality**. In other words, a project that met pre-established quality objectives was defined as successful.

Later, in the **1980s**, a successful project was defined when, in addition of meeting quality requirements, it met **deadlines and budget** according to the project plan.

Starting in the **1990s**, it was not enough to meet the quality, deadlines, and budget to achieve a successful project. Moreover, it was necessary that the project achieves the "**customer's satisfaction**". What would be the point of a project of an exceptional quality, reaching the deadlines with pre-established resources, if nobody buys the products of that venture after its completion?

We should also add to these four characteristics of a successful project the "**sustainability or care**". That is, we could not define as successful a project that met technical quality parameters, schedule, budget and customer satisfaction, if we were not able to preserve the environment or the team members during project execution. For example, if the project was too demanding in order to meet its technical parameters that every team member was physically worn out and/or angry, surely we will not be able to use these people on similar projects. Therefore, the definition of a successful project could be overshadowed.

Therefore, up until the date of writing this book, we can say that a project to be **successful**, it should meet at least the following requirements:

- ✓ **Budget**
- ✓ **Deadlines**
- ✓ **Quality**
- ✓ **Client's Acceptance**
- ✓ **Sustainability**

1.2   PROJECT FAILURES

There are thousands of project failures that did not meet some of the parameters mentioned earlier. Let us see some examples.

Sydney's **Opera House** is a project that most Australians are very proud of, and if they had the opportunity, would do it again, because it generates a good tourist income.

However, from the standpoint of the technical definition of success, we cannot say that it was successful. Based on the original budget, they estimated an investment of $7 million dollars, and the project finished with an investment of $107 million dollars. It is clear that this $100 million dollar miscalculation places this project on the list of unsuccessful projects for not meeting the **budget**.

The **Eurotunnel** is one of the thousands of projects that did not meet the **schedule**.

Based on the plan, it was supposed to be delivered in 1992. However, it had a two-year delay, opening its doors to the public in 1994.

Not only that, but it had budget issues as well, because time is money. Based on an initial estimated investment of $7,500 millions of dollars, the project was completed with an investment of $17,500 millions of dollars. That $10,000 million dollars deviation was a sunk cost (and very well sunken under all that water!) those investors will not be able to ever recover with the project's operation.

The **Tacoma Narrow** Suspension Bridge, also known as the "Galloping Gertie" because of its strong undulations when strong winds were present on the area, is an excellent example of failure by not meeting **quality**.

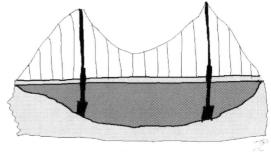

The technicians were worried about perfectly meeting the schedule and the budget, which they met without any inconvenience.

In regards to quality, they had planned the bridge to withstand winds of up to 120 miles per hour. However, one day with the wind only reaching 40 miles per hour, the bridge started vibrating and violently undulating causing its complete destruction. This catastrophe occurred only 4 months after its official inauguration in 1940, which put an end to the world's third longest bridge up to that point.

Why worrying too much about the budget and the schedule, if we neglect quality?

The **Concorde** was an airplane designed to fly faster than the speed of sound.

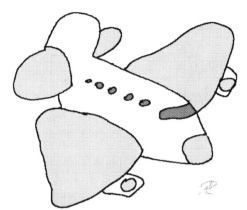

The technology used was admirable; the airplane traveled the London – New York route in less than 4 hours.

There were so many businesses between those two cities that everybody thought it would be a huge commercial success.

For example, an entrepreneur living in one of those cities, could travel to the other city for a meeting and come back to sleep at home on the same day.

However, the project never achieved "**customer satisfaction**". To achieve its breakeven point, the airfare for that route had to be sold at a minimum of $8,000 with the airplane full of passengers. Apparently, they never found enough people that wanted to do business at such a high price and in October 2003, the project closed its doors.

In 1986, during the project for the energy shutdown drill at **Chernobyl**, occurred one of the biggest **environmental disasters** in history.

The explosion at the nuclear plant killed 33 people and contaminated at least another 600,000 with nuclear radiation. Up to this date, it is not clear how many deaths can be attributed to that great project failure.

Even though the project were under budget and on time, it is clear that this wasn't a very successful shutdown project.

1.3   EVOLUTION OF GOOD PRACTICES

In order to improve the project´s efficiency to be closer to those that are successful, rather than the ones that fail, the world has seen a great evolution of good practices.

If we take as a reference the last 100 years, the first drastic change in the way projects were managed started in the **1920s** with the teachings of Henry Ford and his **mass production** model.

Mass Production	Total Quality	Six Sigma	Lean / Agile
1920 - 1960	1960 - 1985	1985 - 1995	1995 - ...

During the "Ford" era, efficiency and productivity were improved greatly by aligning productive processes with specialization and the division of labor, so each company department would specialized in what they knew how to do best. These concepts were previously taught by the American economist Frederick Taylor.

Before the Taylor / Ford era, each worker was responsible of planning and executing their projects, with freedom to do activities in the way they thought most appropriate. They were not organized by areas of specialization, because it was wrongly thought that the person in charge or boss knew how to do things much better than the combined sum of its subordinates.

Nowadays, many of the mass production concepts from the 20s are still deeply rooted in some companies, who maintain rigid **functional departments** in the management of their projects.

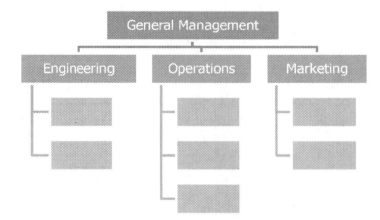

The other change occurs approximately in **1960**, when people start paying more attention to project´s quality management processes. The era of **total quality** had arrived, when managing any project relating to mass production.

These processes came hand in hand with a **matrix organization**, rather than independent functional departments. Some companies started developing a new functional department called Project Management Office (PMO), or at least started to assign Project Managers with enough authority to utilize resources from the different company departments when executing projects.

It was clear that there were more chances of having a successful project working with a matrix structure, rather than being stuck with independent functional departments.

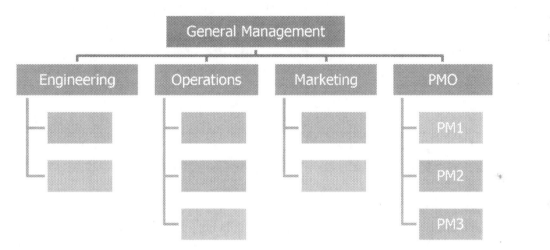

Starting in **1985**, Motorola started the concept of **"Six Sigma"**, where companies had to keep improving the efficiency of their quality management processes. For example, if the company was dedicated to the production of goods and services, it could only have one defect every one million good or service that hit the market.

In this era, the concept of **Concurrent Engineering** was proposed so not only the Project Manager worked with different members of the organization in a matrix structure, but it was also convenient to include top management in key decisions about the project, to avoid the constant changes that projects suffered.

An important milestone of this era happens when the Project Management Institute, the world's largest nonprofit organization dedicated to project management , launches the first edition of the **PMBOK**® Guide [1], where it is clear that to achieve a successful project it is not enough to focus just on quality. On the contrary, planning and project management has to be done including integrated processes from different knowledge areas: scope, time, cost, quality, human resources, communications, risks, procurement and integration.

Around **1995**, the concept of "**Lean**" emerges due to the excellent processes that Toyota was implementing in its projects. These concepts were quickly applied in the rest of the world, and companies start improving the efficiency in their processes.

The world recognized that working in projects with formal processes was important, but if these processes were delaying projects´ schedules, it was necessary to polish or eliminate those processes that were not necessary.

Companies started developing projects where they need to find a smart balance between "processes and control" vs. "speed and customer value". They seek to maintain a **continuous flow** of customer value without interruptions.

Although all good practices developed up to that point were excellent for mass production, sometimes they had more processes than necessary, slowing down projects and neglecting the client.

Lean concepts arrive to remove all those excesses in programming, to focus on delivering value to the customer as soon as possible.

In **2001**, a group of computer engineers from Utah, USA, writes the **Agile** Manifesto for the software development project management community.

---

[1] Project Management Body of Knowledge. PMBOK® is a registered trademark of the Project Management Institute, Inc.

These concepts quickly become popular worldwide and they start being applied not only for software development, but also, for any type of projects.

What is behind these Lean and Agile philosophies?

How can those concepts help us in managing any type of project, even if we don't belong to mass production or software development?

In order to answer these questions, unfortunately, you will have to keep reading the rest of this book. ☺

1.4   TYPES OF TIMES

Like it or not, somebody defined that one day has 24 hours. This is defined as **"calendar time"**.

Out of those 24 hours, how many hours can we work on average? 8, 10, 12, … 18? It doesn't matter what the answer is, the time that we work every day is called **"time worked"**.

Finally, the time related with the Lean philosophy is the **"value added time"**. In order to understand this concept, let us suppose that a hidden video camera has been put in our office and our client is observing everything that we do. The value added time includes only those activities that our client is willing to pay for… surely a lot less than the time worked.

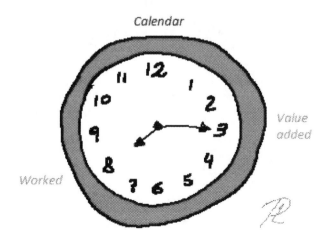

📖 Exercise 1 – Value added time

Mary Smith is an economist that is working on the definition of a huge investment project. Her task is to develop the market research that will later be used to forecast the project's cash flow.

<u>Mary</u>: *I have been working very long hours on this project for the past two weeks and I have not make significant progress. What is happening? Why do I have such low productivity?*

Worried about her slow progress on the project, Mary reviews in detail what she did during her last 10-hour working day.

Suppose you are Mary and complete the following table with the value added time.

Activity	Start	Finish	Value added minutes
Coffee, newspaper, talking, etc.	8:00	9:00	
Project status meeting	9:00	10:00	
Planning meeting	10:00	11:00	
Call from a talkative client	11:00	12:00	
Request the same information once again	12:00	13:00	
Lunch	13:00	14:00	
Skype, emails, twitter, LinkedIn, Google+	14:00	15:00	
Domestic tasks: school, kids, bank, etc.	15:00	16:00	
Statistical Analysis for the project	16:00	17:00	
Lost work due to not saving changes	17:00	18:00	
TOTAL	**10 hours**		

✋ Take 10 minutes to answer before moving on with the reading.

📖 Answers – Exercise 1

Remember that value added time is only the time that the client is willing to pay for. It doesn't matter if what we do is good or bad, productive or unproductive, only if the client pays or not.

After doing this exercise with thousands of executives from important companies in more than 20 countries, we have taken one of the many responses received as an example. This response doesn't mean that it is correct or incorrect; it is just one example, a very real example of what happens in our projects.

Activity	Start	Finish	Value added minutes
Coffee, newspaper, talking, etc.	8:00	9:00	0
Project status meeting	9:00	10:00	20
Planning meeting	10:00	11:00	20
Call from a talkative client	11:00	12:00	10
Request the same information once again	12:00	13:00	0
Lunch	13:00	14:00	0
Skype, emails, twitter, LinkedIn, Google+	14:00	15:00	10
Domestic tasks: school, kids, bank, etc.	15:00	16:00	0
Statistical Analysis for the project	16:00	17:00	60
Lost work due to not saving changes	17:00	18:00	0
TOTAL	**10 hours**		**120**

Generally, that first hour in the morning when we start our day with general lectures, coffee, office talks, and many others that have no relation to our projects whatsoever, tends to be of 0 value added.

When the moment comes for meetings, we tend to be very inefficient. For example, we never start at the scheduled time because we wait for everybody to arrive to the meeting. We also don't talk specifically about our project, because we mix other topics throughout the agenda, or we go over the same topic many times, etc. To put 20 minutes of value added time in those meetings planned for an hour, is being honest with the client.

When that talkative client calls us, he should hire a psychologist instead of a project manager; and to make it even worse, we don't charge by the hour. It could have happened that instead of the whole hour that we spent on the phone, we could have invested it on a concise 10-minute talk focused specifically on our project.

Request the same information that already should be in our desk ready to be worked is, without a doubt, a 0 value added activity. It would be good to discover a formula for requesting information only once, without having to repeatedly roam through the company halls until getting what we need.

Midday we got hungry and it is necessary to recover energy with a lunch that clears our mind. That lunch hour is very necessary, even if the client doesn't pay for that time.

After lunch, we catch up with emails and social networks. However, there were very few topics related to the project during that hour.

Next, we do multiple domestic tasks that every mortal needs to tend to. Unfortunately, our client is not willing to pay for that hour either.

We already have been working for 8 hours in the office, and we have realized that very little time was focus on the project. Therefore, we have decided to disconnect from the email and all social networks, we turned off the cell phone, ask our assistant to not transfer any calls, and we concentrate only in working on our project. Thanks God, a whole value added hour appears without interruptions.

After 9 hours of work, we are so tired that our mind's hard disk starts to be very unproductive. After one hour in which we thought we were working, due to an oversight and overtiredness, we lost all the work performed. Without a doubt, the client will not pay for that error. Surely next day, starting well rested, we could do the same thing in a few minutes.

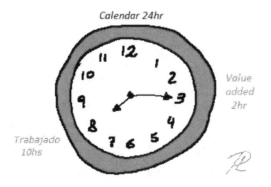

Calendar 24hr

Value added 2hr

Trabajado 10hs

It doesn't matter if you got different results from this example that we just shared. The important thing is that surely your value added time tends to be far fewer than the time worked, and that is the key message that we should take from this exercise.

Continuing with Mary's example, she only had 120 minutes of value added time in a 10-hour workday. If instead of 10 hours, the exercise had been for a typical 8-hour workday, we would have gotten approximately 96 minutes of value added time.

10% of 96 minutes are 9.6 minutes, in rounded numbers, 10 minutes.

If this book helps us discover an idea to add an **additional 10% of value added time** to what we do every day, in other words, 10 additional minutes daily, those daily 10 minutes could be translate into the following:

- To perform **10% more projects** with the same resources.
- To obtain **10% increase in profitability** with the same resources.
- To work **10% faster** in the projects, without adding any costs or neglecting quality.

We invite you to keep looking for throughout this book the reasons we keep adding so little value time in our day to day, and what we can do to improve this situation.

1.5 DISTORTIONS TO ADD VALUE

There are hundreds of inefficiencies in our projects that explain why we obtain so little value added time, in relation to our time worked.

Next, we mention some of these problems, which will be covered in depth throughout this book.

- **Lack of information**: if we don´t have all the information, it is likely that we will not understand the client's needs, or that we may be working on a project´s version that no longer makes sense.

- **Change of priorities**: if the project changes priorities permanently, without being requested and previously approved by the client, we are surely generating very little value added time.

- **Wait in lines**: Why was I invited to a meeting where I sat for two hours without participating, and where my topic was covered on the last 10 minutes of the meeting? Why was I left unattended on the door for half an hour before assisting me? All those unnecessary wait times don't add value.

- **Firefighting**: When we have voluntary firefighter structures on our project teams, who only work in emergency cases, we face serious problems to add value every day in a proactive manner. These firefighters work with a reactive scheme of putting out the fire when it is already on top of us, which is not beneficial to the project and the client.

- **Lack of resources**: If we don't have resources available in a timely manner, the project will advance a lot slower than necessary, delivering less value to the client.

- **Multi-tasks**: We have to understand that it is impossible to work with more than one project at the same time. For instance, we can't be the quarterback and the wide receiver at the same moment, either we throw or we catch the ball! Multi-tasking tends to be a detriment to adding value to the client.

📖 Sitting for 8 hours in front of your computer thinking, and developing the report during the last hour, what was the value added time: 1 or 8 hours?

✋ Take 2 minutes to think the response before moving on with the reading.

Some people answer this question with 1 hour, because the rest would not be time that the client would pay if we had a hidden camera watching us. Others answer 8 hours, because the client also tends to pay for us to think for the best way to do things. Finally, some answer values between 1 and 8, considering that thinking for 7 hours is excessive and the same thing could be done in less time.

It doesn't make sense to advance with this book discussing topics like:

> How much value added time corresponds to thinking?
> How can I add more value in my thoughts?
> How do we make our client understand that thinking is also value added time?

Instead, we consider more productive to dedicate our precious time discussing those issues where it is certain that there is no value added time from the client's perspective. Topics like:

- ✓ Sitting in unnecessary **meetings**
- ✓ Requesting **information** repeatedly
- ✓ Make mistakes and do **re-work**
- ✓ Obtain multiple **bureaucratic** approvals in order to advance with the project

In the next chapter, we will develop what is behind the Lean and Agile thinking, from the perspective of improving first those activities where we generate little or no value added.

LESSONS LEARNED

A successful project is the one that meets the budget, schedule, quality, customer satisfaction and sustainability.

Good practices evolved from mass productions with functional departments, going through the quality management processes with matrix structures, currently searching for a continuous flow of customer value with the lean and agile philosophies.

The value added time the client is willing to pay for, tends to be far fewer than the time worked. This is due to inefficiencies like: lack of information, permanent changes in priorities, unnecessary waits, lack of resources, multi-tasking, etc.

2 LEAN THINKING

Good writers are those who keep the language efficient. That is to say, keep it accurate, keep it clear.

EZRA LOOMIS POUND. (1885-1972)
U.S. poet, critic

Lean Thinking, Lean Production, Lean Manufacturing, Lean Project Management, or simply **"Lean"**, is a school of thought that considers any type of cost that has no relation with adding value to the customer, is waste that should be eliminated.

As seen on the previous chapter, "value" is anything that the client is willing to pay for.

The Lean technique makes reference to a management philosophy born in the 1990s in the Japanese automotive industry, principally at Toyota, hence it is still known as "Toyotism". It is about a simple work organization and project management system, which is also based on a simple principle: **preserve customer value while working less**, by eliminating waste!

Lean thinking consists of a series of methods and tools focused on:

- ✓ **Eliminate losses** due to delays and inefficiencies in the organization's processes,
- ✓ Prevent and **eliminate failures**, interruptions, and other operational losses,
- ✓ Search for perfection and quality **improvements** on a continuous basis.

The Lean philosophy can be summarized in five **fundamental principles**:

1. Specify the **value** of each project with precision
2. Identify the project's value **stream**
3. Allow value to **flow** without interruptions
4. Allow the **client** to participate in identifying "value"
5. **Continuously** search for perfection

2.1 SPECIFY THE VALUE

Putting yourself on the Client's shoes to evaluate if an activity adds value is a critical test of any activity. The Client pays for things that are believed to add value. This is a whole lot different than thinking they buy the things that we consider valuable.

 "**Value**" can be considered anything that the client is willing to pay for. Any activity that does not increment the price that the client would pay, only adds costs to the project.

Activities with no value can fall into two categories:

Type 1 Waste: are activities with little or no value added, and although the client would not pay for them, we should keep doing them because they are necessary to have a successful project. For example, perform a project charter, a progress meeting, a quality audit process, etc.

Type 2 Waste: are non-value added activities that should be eliminated. Japanese call them "muda" or rotten fruits. For example, shorten the time lost in meetings, eliminate obsolete bureaucratic processes, reduce errors and re-work, etc.

📖 Exercise 2 – Wastes

Larry O'Dowell, a sales representative for a knife company, complains about the loss of an important client.

<u>Larry</u>: *I can't believe it. Our knives not only have the best quality, but also have the best packaging and presentation of the market. How come our client chose our competitor's knives that don't have any kind of packaging, or case, or nothing, and they charged the same price as ours!*

Although that company always packed and presented its knives with the best case in the market, they had never asked their clients about their thoughts on that added value. From the client's perspective, knives without a case were more convenient in order to avoid paying overweight when exporting them to other countries. The client, every time they bought those knives, had to dedicate resources to take out and discard the cases.

In order to understand value from the client's perspective, we will group project activities in three categories:

- **Value**: anything that the client is willing to pay for.
- **Type 1 Waste**: activity with little or no value added, but necessary to complete tasks. They add costs to the project, without directly affecting its price.
- **Type 2 Waste**: non-value added. They are "rotten fruits" or "muda" that should be eliminated.

Our objectives are to eliminate type 2 wastes and then attack those aspects that don't add value in activities with type 1 wastes.

Mark with an X to which category belongs each activity

Activity	Value	Waste	
		Type 1	Type 2
Conduct a weekly meeting to manage the team			
Follow up on information requested last month that was not delivered			
Project status report presentation to management			
Creation of official documents not requested by the client			
Obtain multiple approvals for a progress document			
Wait in lines to obtain resources			
Obtain government permits for the start of the project			

✋ Take 10 minutes to answer before moving on with the reading.

📖 **Answers - Exercise 2**

After conducting this exercise with thousands of executives grouped in teams of 4 to 6 people, we have based our example on the response of the majority.

This response doesn't mean that it is correct or incorrect, it is only an example, whose main focus is to evaluate if there is consensus between the members of a team to start eliminating waste and inefficiencies on our projects.

Activity	Value	Waste	
		Type 1	Type 2
Conduct a weekly meeting to manage the team		X	
Follow up on information requested last month that was not delivered			X
Project status report presentation to management		X	
Creation of official documents not requested by the client		X	
Obtain multiple approvals for a progress document			X
Wait in lines to obtain resources			X
Obtain government permits for the start of the project	X	X	X

Most of the respondents answered that conducting a project meeting tends to be an activity for which the client doesn't pay, but it is necessary for the project execution.

Following up on information many times until getting it tends to be a real waste that we should improve.

Present the project status report internally and the creation of official documents, also tend to be activities for which the client doesn't pay, but necessary to have a chance of a successful project.

Obtain multiple bureaucratic approvals in order to advance to the next phase of the project, tends to be an excess. Shouldn't we be able to get the same control with a little less bureaucracy?

Waiting in line for my turn is inefficient and it doesn't add value.

Obtaining a government permit tends to be the item most discussed. Some say that it is "value" because the client pays for those lobbying services; others say that it is "type 1 waste" because it must be done even if the client doesn't pay. Finally, others say that it is "type 2 waste" because it is an unnecessary bureaucracy that the government has created only to employ public officials.

No matter which was your response to this exercise, the important thing is to get consensus with your project team about the wastes that you are facing.

Contrary to what other authors think, the simplest way to start introducing a "lean" culture in projects is to **start with simple things** that don't face much opposition from the rest of the organization. Don't try to start with enhancements that we think will add lots of value to the client, but let's take the first steps with those wastes that everybody agrees can be eliminated.

2.2 DEFINE THE VALUE STREAM

Now that we are clear on what value and waste are, we have to identify what are the value points that the project generates throughout time.

This value stream is composed of all the necessary tasks that must be completed to deliver the product or service to the client. Most of the tasks that we take on, don't add any additional value to the client for what they would be willing to pay for.

Creating a value stream "map", we can easily identify the tasks that add value from those that do not.

Tasks that don't add value for the client are considered waste and should be eliminated from the value stream. Meanwhile, some tasks are wastes, but necessary to complete the project on a timely manner. The last objective of the Lean thinking will be **to eliminate as much "muda" from the value stream as possible**.

However, how do we identify the value stream of a project?

Every set of activities should have a deliverable, and every deliverable should have a client (internal or external). Generally, if we focus on the project **deliverables**, we will be building the value stream.

For example, next we present a simple Gantt chart of a project with 14 activities. However, many of those activities are "type 1 waste", and the deliverables for which the client is willing to pay for, are just a few.

Task	Duration	Jan	Feb	Mar	Apr
Software project	**105 days**				
Contract Approval	**20 days**				
Generate proposal	20 days				
Negotiation meetings	15 days				
Contract Revision	**15 days**				
Finish execution plan	15 days				
Revision meetings	7 days				
Project Definition	**20 days**				
Risk Analysis	20 days				
Meetings with client	10 days				
Software implemented	**30 days**				
Data search	15 days				
Database configuration	30 days				
Equipment search	10 days				
Testing	10 days				

If we only graph the value stream, with those deliverables for which the client is willing to pay for, our project would be simplified to the following way:

Value	Duration	Jan	Feb	Mar	Apr
Contract approval	20 days				
Contract revision	15 days				
Project definition	20 days				
Software implemented	30 days				

If we had a project with thousands of activities, surely just a few of them will be part of the value stream.

Summarizing, this #2 principle asks us to focus on the different value points that the project generates throughout time, without including any type 1 waste and eliminating any type 2 wastes.

2.3 VALUE FLOWS WITHOUT INTERRUPTIONS

Once we have designed the project value stream, the #3 principle tells us that we have to allow for that **"value" to reach the client as fast as possible**. We should stop putting up obstacles that delay deliverables for the client.

The traditional process in the production of goods and services has been constructed on a serial base with lines and waiting times. With the "lean" philosophy, we should take a different path, focusing on the client and accelerating the value stream designed to satisfy their needs.

"Muda" must be eliminated from the value stream and the waiting period for the delivery of the product or service must be reduced.

This means that we must reduce the delay times on the value stream by taking out unnecessary obstacles in the process. We must repair the original flow and achieve a continuous product movement throughout the value stream.

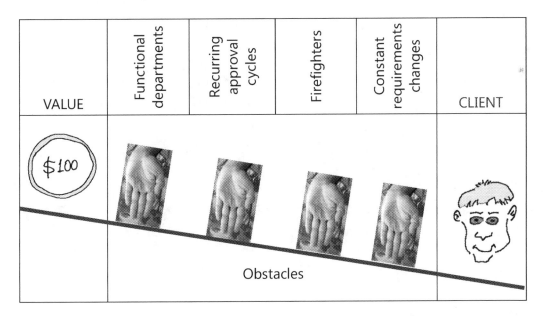

Remove obstacles from the beginning of the project will allow us to:

- ✓ Free up spaces
- ✓ Reduce stocks
- ✓ Change inefficient processes
- ✓ Understand that employees cannot be multi-functional

Some of the typical obstacles to remove from the value stream are:

- ✓ Stiffness of **functional departments**
- ✓ Recurring approval **cycles**
- ✓ Voluntary **firefighters** that only put out fires
- ✓ **Constant changes** in project requirements
- ✓ Etc., etc., etc.

Why is it so hard to remove obstacles that impair the speed of the project's value stream?

Let's look to the following case in order to understand that in some situations we don't remove obstacles, simply because we don't want to.

Case India - Paradigm for not changing

In India, when they don't want an elephant to move from its place, they simply tie a chain with a stone to its leg. The elephant has much more force than the stone's weight, so it could move without a problem. However, if the elephant saw the stone on its leg, it will not even try to move.

How did the Hindu achieve this?

When the elephant is a newborn, they tie that chain and stone to its little leg. The little elephant tries to move, but has no success. From that moment, it lives its life with the paradigm that if they put that stone on its leg, it will not be able to move, and it will not even tried to remove that obsolete obstacle.

Conclusion: Let's try to remove the stones from our projects. Something that at some point was necessary on our organization, it may have probably turned into "muda" and we may have to eliminate it.

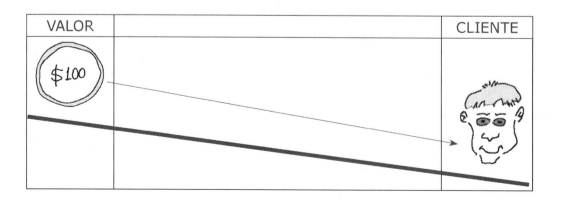

2.4 THE CLIENT PARTICIPATES IN VALUE

The #4 principle of lean thinking reminds us that we have to invite the client to participate on the definition of what adds value to the project.

Sometimes teams tend to be arrogant, thinking that they know more than the client and that they will be able to solve all their needs without consulting with them.

In more than one opportunity, projects were formulated only by a team of experts, without any client intervention. As a result, they ended up with products or services that did not have a market.

Case Cuba – Cigarette without smoke

The Nabiz Company had invested hundreds of millions of dollars to develop a cigarette that will produce no smoke. What an excellent idea! That product would be used in public places, airplanes, offices, schools, etc. The product would only cause cancer to the person smoking it, but without harming others with the smoke.

But what did the clients say when the product was completed?

The clients that tried the cigarette said that it tasted like shit and it smelled like a fart. In addition, they were really hard to inhale, something the experts called the "hernia effect".

During the research and development process, the company experts had little contact with the end user, which it surely was a bad play on their part.

Conclusion: There is no point in doing well what it is useless. It is the client who needs to guide the experts in identifying what adds value to the project.

Project teams should **allow their clients to help them identify what adds value**.

For example, going back to exercise #2, about the company that manufactured knifes with the best packaging in the market; they never asked their clients their opinions about those case boxes. If they had asked, they would find out that those cases were not worth one single penny. The producer would have saved lots of costs and unnecessary processes, the client wouldn't have move to their competitors, and both would have earn more money.

We also need to remind our experts that technology in itself doesn't add up value, but only what that technology is capable to solve focusing on our client needs.

Case USA – Apple's Newton

One of the first pocket tablets ever launched was the Apple's Newton in 1993.

The product had lots of functionality for the users of that time. However, it was considered a commercial failure because of the low sales. The product was designed by, and only for computer engineers, without consulting much with end users along the product development.

In 1995, Palm Inc. decided to ask the users about what it was that they did not like about Apple's excellent product. The response was that it was "too big". With that concept in mind, the technicians eliminated lots of functionality in the product to create the Palm Pilot, which was simply a personal organizer, and the product was a huge success.

The rematch came in 2010, when Apple launched the successful iPad, which revolutionized the industry. Part of its development was based on the Newton, but this time with the clear concept of understanding that not all clients have the same tastes as the developers.

Conclusion: delivering technology on itself doesn't add value to the client. Only when new methods or ideas solve a well-defined problem for the client, is when they add value.

We should only build what our client needs, when it needs it. Using this approach, we should allow our client to schedules our agenda and guides us on what we have to do.

2.5 CONTINUOUSLY SEARCH FOR PERFECTION

The last principle of lean thinking tells us that once we have managed to introduce a lean culture within our projects, it is necessary to **keep improving on a continuous basis**. Otherwise, we will suffer the Entropy Law, which indicates that things in this world tend to go back to their natural chaotic state by themselves.

For example, if on Monday we want to start the week with our desk very neat and clean, surely we have to put some effort on putting everything in its place and clean. Once everything is impeccable, we start with the day-to-day of our office tasks. If during the week we don´t do anything else about the cleaning, by Friday that desk will surely be back to being as messy as it was on Monday.

The same thing can happen to our projects. Everything that we do to introduce a lean culture can be lost if we don´t keep improving on a daily basis.

There are many projects that have created incredible products, in record time, and at a minimum cost. However, sooner or later they could get distracted and go back to the more traditional cycles of start-stop-start-stop...

A lean project requires constant monitoring to maintain and improve its performance, demands team discipline, a **total intolerance towards resource waste, and the constant search for perfection**.

LESSONS LEARNED

The lean philosophy tells us that we have to add value through the elimination of inefficiencies. This can be achieved by keeping in mind these five principles:

1. Distinguish the difference between value (anything that the client is willing to pay for) and wastes (type 1 if we have to keep doing it or "muda" if it's something unnecessary).

2. Build up the project's value stream throughout time, eliminating all the "muda" from that stream.

3. Remove those obstacles that don't allow us to quickly deliver value to the client.

4. Interact with the client so they can express if there is value or not on the project. Don't leave the definition of value 100% to the technicians or "experts".

5. Continuously search for perfection to avoid the Entropy Law, where every project improvement could go back to their natural state of inefficiency.

3 THE AGILE MANIFESTO

Simplicity is the ultimate sophistication.

LEONARDO DA VINCI. (1452-1519)
Polymath.

In honor of the agile movement, we will keep this chapter very short.

3.1 THE MANIFESTO

On February 2001, a group of engineers met in Utah to write the Agile Manifesto, because they had many problems when managing information systems projects with the traditional practices existing up to that moment.

And in a simplified manner they wrote the following:

We are uncovering better ways of developing
software by doing it and helping others do it.
Through this work we have come to value:

Individuals and interactions *over processes and tools*
Working software *over comprehensive documentation*
Customer collaboration *over contract negotiation*
Responding to change *over following a plan*

That is, while there is value in the items on
the right, we value the items on the left more.[2]

---

[2] http://agilemanifesto.org

Individuals and interactions: If we pay close attention to putting together a good project team and to human relations between them, we will obtain a better result than when implementing all the processes and tools that the manuals tell you. For example, do we have to apply all of the processes in the PMBOK®

Guide, a manual of good practices about project management, to all of our projects?[3] The answer is absolutely NOT. If we would apply all processes, all the time, projects would turn very sluggish and bureaucratic. But it is very important to know all of the project management processes, in order to know which one of those apply to each particular project.

Working software: Rather than to write multiple pages explaining a project's progress report, or when will we make it work, or what is the estimated percentage of progress; it is preferable to see if the software is working or not, and dedicate the scarce resources to make it work, instead of writing testaments explaining it.

Customer collaboration: Is it worth being continuously negotiating contract terms? Does it add value to refer conflicts to each party's legal department? It is better to recognize that there are no perfect contracts and that each part

may have made mistakes redacting and/or interpreting it. If we understand that our client is a strategic partner and we achieve to maintain a fluid relationship based on collaboration, projects will end faster and with more value, in relation to allocating scarce resources to contracting fights.

Responding to change: There are two truths in life: all of us are going to die, and there is no project that ends in exactly the same way that the original plan said. We have to understand that the perfect plan doesn't exist. In addition, the context changes permanently, and if we want to execute the project exactly as the plan says, many times we will crash the project. Hence, we have to be flexible to the changes that the client needs.

---

[3]   PMBOK is a registered mark of the Project Management Institute, Inc.

3.2   PRINCIPLES

The four values behind this Agile Manifesto also have their **12 principles**: [4]

1. *Our highest priority is to satisfy the customer through early and continuous delivery of valuable software.*
2. *Welcome changing requirements, even late in development. Agile processes harness change for the customer's competitive advantage.*
3. *Deliver working software frequently, from a couple of weeks to a couple of months, with a preference to the shorter timescale.*
4. *Business people and developers must work together daily throughout the project.*
5. *Build projects around motivated individuals. Give them the environment and support they need, and trust them to get the job done.*
6. *The most efficient and effective method of conveying information to and within a development team is face-to-face conversation.*
7. *Working software is the primary measure of progress.*
8. *Agile processes promote sustainable development. The sponsors, developers, and users should be able to maintain a constant pace indefinitely.*
9. *Continuous attention to technical excellence and good design enhances agility.*
10. *Simplicity, the art of maximizing the amount of work not done, is essential.*
11. *The best architectures, requirements, and designs emerge from self-organizing teams.*
12. *At regular intervals, the team reflects on how to become more effective, then tunes and adjusts its behavior accordingly.*

If we pay close attention to the first principle, there is close similarity to the lean philosophy: "client", "value", and "continuous stream".

On the other hand, the last principle is also similar to what lean says: "continuous improvement".

---

[4]   http://agilemanifesto.org/principles.html

3.3 TENDENCIES

Currently, this "agile" thinking movement is more popular than the "lean" philosophy, but we could say they are similar in many points.

Behind agile thinking there are many tools or techniques specific for managing software projects, like for example:

- ✓ Adaptive Software Development
- ✓ Crystal
- ✓ Dynamic systems development method (DSDM)
- ✓ Extreme Programming
- ✓ Feature-Driven Development
- ✓ **Kanban** – Appendix C
- ✓ Pragmatic Programming
- ✓ **Srum** – Appendix B
- ✓ Etc., etc., etc.

It is not the purpose of this book to enter into detail about these techniques for agile software project management.

Instead, what we will do is to use various concepts from the "lean" philosophy, developed for mass production projects, and from the "agile" philosophy, created for software development projects, to Analyze simple ideas that would allow a more agile management of any type of project.

Before getting to that phase where we will obtain "tips for an agile project", we will discuss on the next part of the book the typical problems and inefficiencies that our projects go through, in other words, the "capital sins".

LESSONS LEARNED

The creators of the agile philosophy invite us to be careful with the traditional concepts like:

- ✓ Strict adherence to processes
- ✓ Strict extensive documentation
- ✓ Endless contractual negotiations
- ✓ Try to always follow the plan verbatim

Instead, they recommend paying close attention to:

- ✓ People and their interactions as a team
- ✓ If the deliverable is completed or not
- ✓ A constant collaboration with the client
- ✓ Respond to changes on the project

PART II

THE CAPITAL SINS

4 TIME BATCHES

Time: is that which a man is always trying to kill,
but which ends in killing him.

HERBERT SPENCER. (1820-1903)
British writer

A time batch is anything that causes delays, but could be avoided, to speed up the project.

The seven capital sins in relation to the time batches in our projects are:

1) Paralysis in decision-making (*Sloth*)
2) Recurrent approval cycles (*Gluttony*)
3) Formality of documentation (*Greed*)
4) Regular meetings (*Anger*)
5) Lines (*Envy*)
6) Owners of the information (*Pride*)
7) A combination of any of the above! (*Lust*)

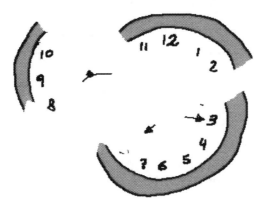

📖 Exercise 3 – Time batches

Anna Richardson is a member of a project team whose task is to perform daily soil tests in a mining project, in order to avoid possible environmental damages.

At the end of each week, Anna saves her samples in a box and sends them to a nearby lab by post mail. The samples sit on the lab for weeks because they work by order of arrival. When they get to the samples, they are routinely tested and the lab sends a report to Ana indicating all the significant risks for each lot relieved during the month.

Anna: *Listen people! We need to accelerate the execution of the project because we are much delayed. We have never had any problems with the soil samples in this region, so let's not delay any further the work by waiting for the lab's report. Let's move on with the drillings.*

However, as usual, Murphy's Law shows up at the least appropriate time. A few weeks before the project's deadline, Anna receives bad news: the samples came up with negative results, which means that the drillings cannot be done.

Unfortunately, some drillings should not have been done because the samples did not meet the minimum environmental requirements. Worst, there are many other samples waiting in line that could also have negative results. All the drillings performed during the previous weeks must be backfilled and covered. The project will finish greatly over budget and with a huge delay.

What are those time batches that could have been avoided?
Order those time batches in chronological order.

🖐 Take 10 minutes to answer before moving on with the reading.

📖 Answer - Exercise 3

You are surely still blaming Anna for the bad decision taken of moving on with the project without waiting for the soil tests results. The truth is that Anna did what many of us would have done in a similar situation, where we never had any problems with the samples and our project would have been in serious problems if we did not accelerate it.

Let's not focus on the risk Anna took. What is important on this exercise is to concentrate on the time batches that most times are the root cause of some of our problems and inefficiencies.

First of all, they are sending the samples to the lab with a weekly frequency, instead of doing it on a daily basis. Therefore, something that could be done in a day, we are making it to last a week.

Second, they are using traditional mail to send the samples, which could be generating an average delay of one week, instead of a few hours if they are delivered personally or with some courier service.

Third, the lab works with the FIFO (First In First Out) system, so samples are not seen until their turn is up. Time starts counting from the day the samples arrived at the lab, and since they have other clients, they usually take a couple of weeks to finish with the other clients and then start with the samples. Perhaps the lab would have accepted an additional fee to review the samples before their other clients, hence receiving the results in a couple of days. Why keep thinking that working with a FIFO system is the most fair?

Last, the lab sends formal written reports on a monthly basis, bundling all weekly lots from the company before producing the reports. Why not ask the lab to call us as soon as they detect a defective sample? Something similar to what an oncologist would do when a tumor is detected. Not much written formality would be needed. With only that single preliminary data of a defective sample given over the phone, we could keep the project on stand-by until we have better information.

Case Puerto Rico - FIFO

A long time ago we took a computer, which was functioning properly, to a company in order to add more memory.

The person that greeted us told us to leave the computer and pick it up in a week.

One week? How is it possible to take that long for something that simple?

No sir, the service that you are asking for only takes 10 minutes, but we have many computers that need repairs before yours. Whenever your turn comes up we will install the memory that you need.

I understand, I will come back next week when you have completed all the pending work and I will then wait 10 minutes for you to add the memory to my computer.

I'm sorry sir, but if you don´t leave your computer you will lose your turn. In addition, next week we will surely have an estimated waiting time of one week or greater.

Conclusion: many companies, doctors, mechanics, consultants, etc., keep working with a FIFO system without any type of rationale. Why not work with a turn system?

Summarizing, a report that could have been delivered in a week, is plagued with many time batches, which caused that Anna found out about the soil problem two months after taking the sample.

With time batches = 2 months

Without time batches = 1 week

In other words, Anna could have found out within a week that she was drilling in a zone with soil risks. To suspend defective work within a week would have cost less and cause much less delays than performing defective work during two consecutive months.

One of the great problems or sins in our projects is that we are working with **time batches** that fill us with inefficiencies, delays, unnecessary work, costs, etc.

4.1 PARALYSIS IN DECISION-MAKING

Sloth is one of the capital sins. That laziness and inability to accept and take charge of things is a problem for the management of our projects.

The paralysis in decision-making is similar to laziness or sloth, and is a permanent time batch.

What do we do next boss? I don't have time now. We'll see it next week. The following week is the same story: *Where do we go boss? I'm still too busy... We'll see it next week.* And the following week, and the following, and the following... the same situation. The project is totally stagnant, hugely delayed, with big complaints from the client, and we cannot progress because of that laziness in making decisions.

Sometimes that lack of decisions is caused by the fear of making a mistake and the associated risk that taking the wrong decision carries with it. But it is worth remembering that in certain situations a **"no decision"** that generates that permanent time batch could be worse than a **"bad decision"**. After all, a bad decision allowed the project to continue and we have a chance of finding a solution to repair that error.

4.2 RECURRENT APPROVAL CYCLES

The overconsumption that is caused by the capital sin **gluttony**, is similar to the excessive approval cycles that delay the progress of a project.

For example, Mary sends a project progress report to Charles for him to review it, approve or disapprove it, in order to move to the next project phase. Charles makes sure to find a few errors, he needed to justify his salary ☺, and he passes the report to Caroline for her revision. Caroline finds errors on Charles' revisions, in addition to other minor changes that she is recommending, and sends the report to Robert's department. Robert comments on the changes made by his three colleagues, and since he has to demonstrate that he is not less than the others, he also adds some of his comments and sends the report with all of the comments back to Mary, who originally sent the document. Mary reviews all the comments, tries to reconcile with the different writing styles and again sends the report to Charles for his approval. Carlos again finds differences with the changes proposed by his colleagues, plus some minor errors that he missed during the first revision. He commented all of this in the report that again sends to Caroline... and Caroline sends to Robert... and Robert sends to Mary... and we start all over again...

Well, this well-known story got too boring, so we better stop with an image of how the **dairy model** is filled with excess and bureaucracies to approve one simple report. This is one of the typical time batches in our projects.

Dairy Model

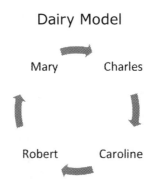

That gluttony for the overconsumption of milk makes us obese, slow, and inefficient! ☺

There are times that the **star** approval model gives us better results and creates fewer delays. In that model, the report is sent to all stakeholders at the same time and all of them have, for example, a week to review it and comment. Then all the comments are reconciled into one final report in order to advance. Whoever did not comment within that week, lost its opportunity.

Star Model

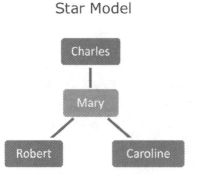

4.3   FORMALITY OF DOCUMENTATION

What is the need of keep waiting to have all the formal project documentation before advancing to the next phase?

This excess **greed** of wanting to gather all formal documentation, with all of the stakeholder's signatures, all departmental official seals, the latest definitive versions, etc., can make us sin in excess, creating a time batch, hence delaying the progress of the project.

Sometimes we want to have all of the formal documentation, waiting until the last second of available time, thinking that this way we will avoid all of the possible changes that the client or sponsor could ask for. This common misconception that waiting until the final moment, gathering signatures and approvals, will be beneficial to the project, is not always correct.

On one hand, in some opportunities we could advance with our activities having preliminary information, never mind that it may not have all the formality that the company policies dictate. For example, due to scheduling conflicts the document has not been signed, but we have been informed by phone that everything is in order to move forward.

On the other hand, although we may have all the formal documentation with its respective seals and original signatures, that will not stop change requests on the next project phases.

4.4   REGULAR MEETINGS

Another meeting? It looks that these guys think that if we are not in a meeting we are not working? Why was I invited to this meeting when none of my topics were covered? Why not leaving more time for me to add value to the project, instead of taking away so much of my time in meetings and more meetings?

This **anger** or hate that the excess of meetings sometimes causes, is because this "meetingitis" sin causes time batches, which delay our projects.

If the project is progressing well, why halt it with periodical scheduled meetings? More than once, on those meetings we get together only to look at ourselves and talk about how good everything is, without any real value exchange for the project or the client.

It is normal to schedule weekly progress meetings during the initial phases of a project. However, once the project advances and those scheduled meetings are not adding so much value, we should think about changing the plan and spread those meetings over longer periods of time. Nevertheless, if at any time the project presents any problems, we must coordinate that meeting as soon as possible, even though the date may not coincide with what was already scheduled.

4.5   WAITING IN LINES

Why my line stopped and everybody else is moving? Why are not those VIP clients in line and I'm still here waiting? Why are they making me waste so much time sitting in that meeting waiting until my turn comes up, and the first ones already finished and they went back to work on the project? Why these closed minded people are keep working with a FIFO system when other colleagues get a turn to come back later?

This **envy** about desiring what other people have, when my line is stopped and everybody else's is moving, frustrates us. Even worst, waiting in lines is another time batch that delays our project.

As we will see later on in one of the commandments in this book (part III), we should try to start working with a turn system, instead of wasting so much time waiting in unnecessary lines.

4.6   INFORMATION OWNERS

Pride, believing that you are better than anybody else, is the principal capital sin.

Some companies have created gurus or owners of the information who believe they are better than anybody else. And to make sure that nobody tries to be like them, they don't share information with the rest of their team.

The owners of the information think: *Information is power, so I will not share it.*

For example, that technological genius that is the only one that knows the passwords to make a software work, that if one day he doesn't show up for work, the rest of the team is delayed with their activities because the computers will not work.

Working in projects with owners of the information is a great sin, because bottlenecks are generated. In other words, time batches, where at some point we end up depending on these people and the project's progress is slower than it could be if information is shared.

Case France – Owner of the Information

Everything was ready to start with the multi-million dollar fiber optics installation project on the historical center of the city. Machines were waiting in order to start digging, hundreds of workers ready to start their activities, and all the resources were ready to start. However, the project was already delayed by two hours and the work was not starting.

What is going on? Why can't we start if everything is ready? *We are waiting for Mr. Joseph,* was the project Manager 's answer.

We were all thinking that Mr. Joseph, Joe to his friends, was the multi-millionaire sponsor that would arrive in his private helicopter to cut the ribbon and take his picture with the international press.

But it wasn't like that. Joe arrived on the train, three hours late. He was a very humble old man, but he was the owner of the information, and that is why everybody had to wait for him.

Joe had installed the gas pipes on that city 50 years ago and he was the only one who knew exactly if the gas lines where on the left or right hand side of the street.

It was worth waiting for Mr. Joe to not drill on the wrong place and avoid explosions. In addition, the international builder was willing to pay a lot of money to Mr. Joe for that valuable information.

Conclusion: Businesses should not award owners of information with good salaries because of all the information they keep to themselves. On the contrary, management mechanisms have to be implemented so project progress doesn't depend on any particular person.

LESSONS LEARNED

The time batches are sins impregnated on our organizations that cause delays in projects that could be avoided. Some of the more common time batches are:

- Paralysis in decision-making: sloth for not advancing, always postponing decisions for later on. The project doesn't advance and sometimes a "bad decision" could be preferable to this chronic state of "no decision".
- Recurrent approval cycles: gluttony for working in excess with multiple bureaucratic approvals, which originate a recurrent cycle without ending, making the project slower.
- Formality of documentation: greed of wanting more and more excessive formal information, instead of advancing with good preliminary information.
- Regular meetings: anger that we feel every time we are invited to a meeting where we don't do anything, we don't add any value to the project, and they unnecessarily take out our scarce time that we could actually spend working on the project.
- Waiting in lines: envy that we feel towards those organizations that manage their time with an efficient turn system, instead of the inefficiency of having to wait in long lines until it is our turn to move forward.
- Owners of the information: pride of those "know it all's" that don't share the information with the rest of the team, which generates bottlenecks and delays the project progress.

The only capital sin that we have not mentioned in this chapter is lust, which means "abundance" or "exuberance". The combination of some of the previous sins becomes some type of lust, which we have to avoid if we want a quick and efficient project.

5 TRANSACTION COSTS

The illusion? That's expensive. It cost me living more than I should have.

JUAN RULFO. (1917-1986)
Mexican novelist

Transaction costs are those project excesses that make it more heavy, and therefore, more expensive and slower.

The majority of type 2 wastes, or muda, easy to identify in projects, are usually found in transaction costs.

The 7 capital sins relating to transaction costs are:

1) Lack of a common language *(Pride)*
2) Excessive formality *(Greed)*
3) Repetitions without an end *(Envy)*
4) Lack of Information *(Sloth)*
5) Excess of information *(Gluttony)*
6) Physical distance between members *(Anger)*
7) Poor communication channel selection *(Lust)*

📖 Exercise 4 – Transaction Costs

Josephine Franz has one week to try to produce a miracle. Three weeks ago, she received the opportunity to work as a project manager for a critical project in her company.

Josephine: I'm going to explain the situation. Our project has a deadline in 30 days to send the proposal to the Client. The good news is that we have the 5 sections almost completed. The bad news is that none of those 5 sections are currently in my hands.

Section 1. Engineering is trying to complete the specifications, but they are being constrained by the actions of the Quality Manager, who always requires that specifications be redone for not complying with small and irrelevant details.

Section 2. The hardware and software engineers cannot agree on the test plan. Josephine setup a meeting, but is seemed as if each group spoke a different language. After long discussions about technical terms and simulations, both parties were not able to understand each other.

Section 3. A junior member of the marketing department, who is right out of college, is doing this section. It seems as if she is still writing an investigation thesis, with complex semantics, lots of poetry, and very little information about the benefits of the product to the client.

Section 4. The representative of each one of the company's international offices was going to provide the required input to develop the global marketing plan. It has been two weeks and they cannot coordinate a meeting, due to the difference in time zones between Kuala Lumpur and Panama.

Section 5. A veteran company expert, who is addicted to emails, is preparing this section. Josephine has called him many times to explain a couple of topics, but since she could not reach him, she leaves voice mails on his phone. However, this expert keeps answering back with emails that are hard to understand.

Having come to this point, Josephine is asking herself...

Josephine: *Why didn't I opt to write the whole proposal by myself? Then if the proposal was rejected, I could've just apologized and that's it!*

Josephine is facing a frustrating paradox. Everything that she needs is available... in the brilliant minds of the team, but the transaction costs are causing the information to never be available on time.

What transaction costs is the project facing?
Could Josephine have done anything to mitigate those costs?

✋ Take 10 minutes to answer before moving on with the reading

📖 Answer - Exercise 4

Section 1 is dealing with the cost of **repetitions without an end**. Every time the report gets to the quality department, the functional manager finds a minor error to fix. Surely, when we fix the error and resubmit the report, a different error will be found. Why didn't he mention all the errors the first time? Could he be envious of the project manager? This is a very complicated solution for the project manager, because in a weak matrix organization she may have less power than the functional manager, who is an expert in finding obstacles to the process. Josephine could try to mitigate this transaction cost by explaining to the Sponsor why it is getting impossible, exhausting, and costly to move on with this section.

Section 2 has the transaction cost related to the **lack of a common language**. Every time that the software guys get together with the hardware band, each one wants to show off their technical pride and doesn't listen, nor wants to learn, the other's language. Josephine should try to put some sort of translator or force a common language, as we will see later on.

Section 3 could be suffering from **excessive formality** by putting hundreds of quotes, references to other authors, and many formalities that are needed in a doctoral thesis, but add little value to a business proposal. Josephine should teach the young worker how to cut the greed of adding more and more formality to the document. For example, she could show her a report done for another client where a maximum of 3 pages were allowed. No doubt there will be no space left for poetry.

Section 4 is constrained by the great **physical distance** that separates the project team members. They are suffering great transaction costs by trying to put together the members of the team. It seems like the distance is angering the teams, which is dividing them even more. Josephine should better plan communications, taking advantage of technology like videoconferencing, to try to shorten that distance.

Section 5 has the cost associated to selecting a **bad communication channel**. This lust of excessively using email is driving Josephine crazy. It is necessary for her to get that face-to-face meeting by all means possible.

5.1   LACK OF A COMMON LANGUAGE

Committing the sin of **pride** by believing that our language is better than the rest of the team's, causes costs to the project. Moreover, if each company division has created their own vocabulary to manage projects; we are in deep trouble.

This lack of a common language in the organization generates great transaction costs that make it difficult to have an efficient project management .

Case Colombia – Common Language

During many years Tecnocolombia.net suffered transaction costs on their projects because software engineers spoke a technical language totally different to the one used by the hardware engineers, despite all of them were working on the same project.

The company had to assign resources to create dictionaries where the terms "x, y, and z" meant exactly the same for the whole organization. In addition, they forced all employees to start using this dictionary, without giving them space for inventing new words for something that was already defined in the dictionary.

Conclusion: communication failures and costs in projects, many times are originated simply for the lack of a common language.

There are many companies investing resources to force a common language within the organization through **dictionaries**. For example, if we look for the meaning of "Project Charter", we could get responses as diverse as:

a) Detailed project plan
b) Gantt Chart
c) Document that authorizes the project existence

If the company wanted to implement a common language for projects, like the glossary terms that is in the PMBOK®, everybody in the organization would know that the term "Project Charter" is referring to option c). A common language is usually achieved through **training**, so it is not necessary to "re-invent the wheel" every time we manage a project.

Moreover, is usually helpful to use **translators** that could facilitate communication whenever there is a language problem. For instance, if we are having communication problems for the creative (soft skills) and the technical (hard skills) to work as a team, we could incorporate a translator who can speak these two languages that appear to be so different. This person could be, for example, an Industrial Engineer who can manage the hard skills, but was softened by an MBA in Human Resources, where he understood that projects are people, not irons; in addition he certified as a PMP® to learn the language and the specific project management processes.

5.2   EXCESSIVE FORMALITY

Control, control, and more controls! Many projects are filled with bureaucratic and excessive control processes, without weighing in, that this **greed** of wanting more and more control generates transaction costs.

We should always think about a rational balance between controls and value stream without interruptions.

For example, if a company wants to lower the monthly costs of photocopies, it could create a process where in order to make a photocopy, a signature and a written justification from three functional departments (Finance, PMO, and Quality) is required. The following month, we would observe that the objective was met, because the costs of photocopies were cut down by more than 50%. However, we are losing sight of the possible million dollar projects that could be getting lost because of not getting a photocopy on time to the client. Wouldn't have been simpler something like: *Anybody making a photocopy for personal reasons not related to the project could be a cause for dismissal!*

Case Brazil – Formalities

H: We are going to start producing in a different way.

F: Excellent idea Henry, but to comply with our internal control processes and advance with the proposal, we need to document the costs that will be saved with that change and send it to the Finance department for its approval.

H: What I am proposing is to save costs. Is Finance not convinced yet?

F: It is very clear that we will save costs. There is no doubt.

H: Then, why waste so much time filling out all the papers to estimate the cost savings? Let's use our scarce time to the re-engineering and after a few months, we will have the exact empirical data of the costs we have saved.

Conclusion: The excess of unnecessary bureaucracy and controls prevent us from advancing in a fast and efficient way.

5.3   REPETITIONS WITHOUT AN END

The excess of controls sometimes has the effect of being trapped in a vicious back and forth cycle that keeps repeating itself, with no end in sight.

For example, when we send a deliverable to a functional department for approval to advance to the next phase, and this department always finds the littlest insignificant error that prevents us from moving forward, that is some serious transaction costs. Worst of all, when we send the deliverable with the change they had asked for, and yet again they find another insignificant error that could have been mentioned on the first revision.

It might seem like functional managers sometimes are **envious** of the possible success of project managers and they make sure to show off their power in order to slow down the project.

We have to understand that in the organization, both functional managers and project managers work for the same team. To achieve a successful project, everybody has to pull the same way by eliminating unnecessarily thorough controls that don´t add value to the client.

Of course we need processes to detect errors and to audit quality, but all improvements should be informed at the same moment. This way, the project team's time is optimized, avoiding those back and forth with no end.

5.4   LACK AND EXCESS OF INFORMATION

Sloth is the inability to take charge of things. That laziness keeps us from gathering all the necessary information to know the client's needs.

The lack of information tends to be a transaction cost, because we produce proposals that are later not accepted by the client.

On the other hand, the sin of **gluttony** takes us to an excess of information overload, which originates over-expenses, miscommunications, and oversized proposals, in relation to what the client needs. In turn, this could cause the client to reject our proposals.

The lack of information could be as bad to the project as the excess of information. It is practically impossible to know precisely what that middle point is, but we have to avoid the extremes if we want to lower transaction costs.

5.5 PHYSICAL DISTANCE

When we get mad with our fellow team members we tend to separate ourselves. The **anger** that separates us makes us communicate less, which originates transaction costs for the project.

Now, not only anger separates us from our colleagues. Many times team members are physically distanced even if their relations are very good.

In the study called "Managing the flow of technology" [5], it was demonstrated that the greater the physical distance between team members, the less is the probability of communication between them. Something obvious, demonstrated with statistics, as summarized in the following graphic.

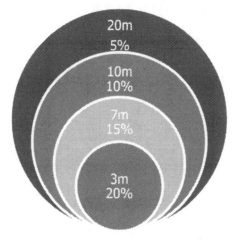

When team members are separated more than 20 meters, the probability of communicating at least once a week is less than 5%. On the other hand, when team members are on the same physical place, only at 3 meters distance, the probability of communicating increases to 20% per week.

Whoever works with agile methodologies, like for example SCRUM, take into account this principle of having the whole team on the same physical place until the deliverable is finished.

But sometimes, having all the team members so close, it could be a little dangerous. For instance, every Friday afternoon they could be planning the recreational activities for the weekend; while Monday morning they could be spending time to find out what was going on during the weekend. ☺

Once again, let´s avoid the extremes, not separated but not so close either! ☺

---

[5]   ALLEN, Thomas J. (1984). Managing the Flow of Technology Transfer and the Dissemination of Technological Information Within the R&D Organization. MIT Press.

5.6 POOR COMMUNICATION CHANNEL SELECTION

Messengers, email, voicemail, website, intranet, voice over IP, cellular, videoconference, Skype, blackberry, Twitter, Facebook, YouTube, LinkedIn, Google+, iPad, iPhone, etc., etc. etc.

Isn't it **lust** (abundance and exuberance) having all these forms of communication?

In addition, every day new communication channels are appearing, which we are learning on the go, because nobody gives us a manual to help us identify which is the best medium or channel for each particular case.

What is the most adequate channel? Hard to know, but we could focus on those who are surely not appropriate.

To identify which communication channel could be less useful, we have to consider the following:

-   Is the communication unidirectional, or bidirectional?
-   How many transmitters-receivers are involved?
-   What bandwidth do we need?

It is worth clarifying that bandwidth is relating to the amount of information, not the megabits or the size of a document. For example, the biggest bandwidth is obtained from a face-to-face meeting.

📖 Exercise 5 – Communication channels

Mark with an X the communication channel that is most used in each of the following project activities:

Activity	Meeting	Phone	e-mail	Intranet	Letter	Documents	Presentation	Others
Work teams coordination								
Collaboration between team members								
Document distribution								
Document revision								
Routine memos								
Detailed project information								
Negotiations								
Formal requests of information								
Team trainings								

🖐 Take **3** minutes to answer before moving on with the reading.

📖 Answers - Exercise 5

There is no best way to communicate, but some recommendations from communication experts could be useful. The next table summarizes some suggestions:

Activity	Involved	Bandwidth	1st Option	2nd Option
Coordination meetings	Few-Few Bidirectional	Medium	Face-to-face	Teleconference
Collaboration meetings	Few-Few Bidirectional	High	Face-to-face	Videoconference
Document distribution	One-Many Unidirectional	Low	Intranet	Email with attachment
Document revision	One-Many Bidirectional	Medium	Email!!	Document
Routine memos	One-One Unidirectional	Low	Email	Document
Detailed project information	One-One Bidirectional	Medium	Document Face-to-face	Email Teleconference
Negotiations	One-One Bidirectional	High	Face-to-face	Videoconference Teleconference
Formal requests of information	One-One Unidirectional	Low	Email w/ digital signature	Formal Letter
Team trainings	One-One Bidirectional	High	Face-to-face	Videoconference

Based on the previous table, the best way to conduct a coordination meeting is face-to-face, with a second option of a teleconference. On the other hand, in a collaboration meeting that requires high bandwidth, the second option should be a videoconference, because even the phone could distort the message.

After doing the previous exercise with thousands of executives from important companies of more than 20 countries, we would like to share the percentages of the responses received. These responses are neither correct, nor incorrect.

For example, 13% of the respondents said that they use email to coordinate the work team. This surely may not be the best communication channel for this project activity, which could be generating transaction costs.

Activity	Meeting	Phone	e-mail	Intranet	Letter	Documents	Presentation	Others
Work teams coordination	77	7	13	0	0	2	1	0
Collaboration between team members	53	15	27	1	0	1	1	1
Document distribution	2	0	64	11	7	11	0	4
Document revision	30	1	31	7	2	22	1	7
Routine memos	0	1	64	4	9	15	1	1
Detailed project information	19	0	23	5	3	27	20	2
Negotiations	85	5	4	0	0	1	3	1
Formal requests of information	2	12	48	1	23	9	1	0
Team trainings	49	1	0	0	0	1	44	4

Some of the conclusions that we could get from these answers and what the communication experts recommend, are that if we want to decrease project transaction costs, we should least try to use those communications channels that are highlighted on the table.

5.7   THE EMAILITIS

On recent years we have observed that the tendency towards the use of email in excess has been getting even stronger. Some people answer the previous exercise #5 by marking email as the only communication channel for all project activities.

We have called these cases of extreme email abuse the *emailitis*, a **sin** in which we are all involved.

How much time of the day are we wasting cleaning our emails? Why would they send us that email that we had nothing to do with? Why do they copy us in everything that happens in the organization? How about those who reply-all with rubbish that fills our mailboxes?

There is no doubt that email is an excellent communication tool that has helped us a lot with the efficiency of our projects. However, like almost all good things in this life, when we sin in excess, we could turn a good thing into a bad thing.

Let's look at some typical **sins** caused by email misuse:

1. Copying everybody, because it is easier to copy everybody, rather than thinking who should really receive the email.

2. Responding the email by copying everybody with silly things like "nice", "yeah", "thanks", etc. Then our colleagues respond copying everybody as well, and all of a sudden, we have hundreds of emails with the same subject on our mailbox.

3. Re-sending an email that has multiple send-receive cycles, where if anybody wants to understand it, it would have to scroll down multiple pages to start reading from the bottom up.

4. Attaching multiple documents on the email, because it is simpler putting all of our documents from our hard drive, rather than thinking which the real critical documents that we should send are.

5. Writing an email with hundreds of lines, to the point of looking more like a testament than a message.

6. Always using the "!" sign of high priority, even though what we are sending is really not "urgent".

Recommendations to lower the transaction costs due to email misuse:

1. Think about whom I should copy. More than three people could be a hint that I'm starting to sin in excess.

2. Don't respond to emails copying everybody.

3. Don't send an email that has already more than two send-receive cycles. In its place, compose a new email with an executive summary of what we want to communicate.

4. Don't send unnecessary attachments.

5. Don't write an email with more than 20 lines. For long topics, write them in a word processor and send it as an attachment.

6. Reserve the "!" sign for real urgent matters.

LESSONS LEARNED

Most of type 2 wastes, which are easy to eliminate, could be found in some of the following project transaction costs:

- Lack of a common language: pride of believing that our technical language is better than the rest. We should use dictionaries, training, and translators to unify the language.
- Excessive formality: greed of wanting more and more controls in projects. We should eliminate this excessive bureaucracy, thinking more about the uninterrupted value stream to the client.
- Repetitions without an end: envy of functional managers towards project managers that keep them from advancing with recurrent approvals with no end. Functional managers and project managers should work as a team.
- Lack and excess of information: sloth for not gathering all the data to really understand the needs of the client; or gluttony for overloading ourselves with information that generate unnecessary costs. Avoid extremes. Both the lack and excess of information are bad for the project.
- Distance: anger that separates team members and make them communicate less. If possible, put project team members as close as possible.
- Poor communication channel selection: lust of abusing the misuse of communication channels. Avoid emailitis and those channels with which surely we will have too much transaction costs.

PART III

THE 10 COMMANDMENTS

So far we have only seen an introduction to the Lean and Agile philosophies and many common sins from our projects, but very few tools or ideas of how to solve those problems.

On the previous section we analyzed the two most frequent problems: time batches and transaction costs, which we explained with a humorous analogy about "capital sins".

These capital sins are nothing but excesses. Fortunately, they always have a virtue to help us overcome them:

On this last Part of the book we are going to focus specifically on ideas to become more **agile** project managers.

For this, we will look at the 10 commandments to become more agile:

I. You shall not add... **wastes** to the project
II. Honor... deliverables to the **client**
III. You shall not lose... time in **meetings**
IV. You shall not forget... the **risk** analysis
V. You shall take away ... **traditional** methods
VI. You shall covet... the **visual** methods
VII. You shall not kill... the standard **processes**
VIII. You shall not provoke... long **waiting lines**
IX. You shall not forget... the critical **resources**
X. Sanctify... **priority** projects

The Ten **Commandments**

I. You shall not add... **wastes** to the project

II. Honor... deliverables to the **client**

III. You shall not lose... time in **meetings**

IV. You shall not forget... the **risk** analysis

V. You shall take away ... **traditional** methods

VI. You shall covet... the **visual** methods

VII. You shall not kill... the standard **processes**

VIII. You shall not provoke... long **waiting lines**

IX. You shall not forget... the critical **resources**

X. Sanctify... **priority** projects

By Paul Leido

6 COMMANDMENT #1

YOU SHALL NOT ADD WASTES TO THE PROJECT

Short as life is, we make it still shorter by the careless waste of time.

VICTOR HUGO. (1802-1885)

French novelist

Many projects don't achieve their objectives simply because they sin with excess of information, unnecessary attributes, or excessive complexity. We will call "wastes" all those unnecessary project extras.

📖 Exercise 6 – Proposals excesses

John Lobby is preparing a project's technical and budget proposal to present to an important client.

John: *How can this be! It's always the same story. What does the client really want? The requirements are too vague and it's practically impossible to interpret the scope of this project. In addition, we have to budget with a fixed fee contract. Therefore, if we add more items than what's necessary, we will not be profitable. On the other hand, if we have less functionality than what the client needs, they will surely select another provider.*

How could John mitigate the risks of sinning in excess when preparing the proposal?

🖐 Take **5** minutes to answer before moving on with the reading.

📖 Answer - Exercise 6

Understanding our clients' needs in order to define the scope of a project tends to be a very hard task.

In some occasions, team members start adding more scope and functionality to the project than what our client really needs. This is a problem, because the client will surely not want to pay for these additions.

On the other hand, we could add less scope than what our client really needs. This is also a problem, because they will not buy our product or service, or we will end up with an unsatisfied client.

On John's case, to not sin in excess when preparing the proposal, he should take into consideration the following techniques or tools:

- Iterative meetings between the client and the team members to specify all the project requirements, and define together the scope of the project.
- Pre-defined surveys that the client must answer to specify their requirements.
- Prepare budgets with scalable modules that specify the price and duration for each deliverable. This way, the client can choose only those modules or deliverables that add value.

6.1 INFORMATION EXCESS

Many projects start adding "add-ons" that are not requested by the client, under the hypothesis that they will surpass expectations and obtain a satisfied customer. However, generally the client will not pay for those add-ons. Therefore, that extras don't add value, could very well add risks, overages and unnecessary delays.

Remember that **we should give our clients what they asked for, no more, no less**.

Like we saw on previous chapters, both the excess (gluttony) and the lack of information (sloth) are a problem. The lack of information could be the cause of not selling our proposal to the client, which generates a loss of profitability. On the other hand, the excess of information makes us work more than necessary, and the client will not pay for those extras either, which also generates a loss of profitability.

What is that optimal point of profitability?

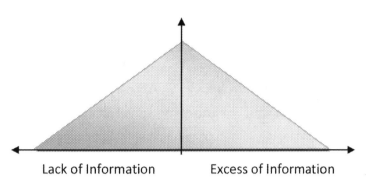

We never know what the optimal level of information that maximizes profitability is, but as usual, the lean-agile project management model invites us to avoid the extremes.

6.2   UNNECESSARY ATTRIBUTES

How many times we keep adding more and more of the same on our projects thinking that is necessary to our clients? Are we sinning in excess by keep adding an unnecessary attribute that the client is not willing to pay for anymore?

For example, the first cell phone launched on the market had the size and the weight of a brick. Without a doubt, research and development on the cell phone industry concentrated on reducing the size and weight of the units. Every time a new smaller model came out, the industry was willing to throw away their old brick and replace it with a smaller and lighter phone.

Would you be willing to throw away the last cell phone that you had in your pocket because a new smaller one just came out?

Neither does us! ☺

These days, to keep investing in research and development to produce smaller cell phones, probably will not significantly increment sales. But investing in new attributes, so our cell phones can look even more like personal computers, could very well be a good strategy.

Something similar occurs with computer processors speed. To add a little more speed to our current computer will surely not give us an incentive to go out and buy the newest model. For example, when Intel launched the Pentium II, it was a commercial failure because it did not add a significant amount of speed, and they had also recently launched its predecessor Pentium I.

Why throw away our Pentium I or pay more for a Pentium II that is not that much faster?, thought consumers on those days.

Meanwhile, adding new functionality, like Apple does when launching a new product, could cause a shortage of the product on its first day on the market.

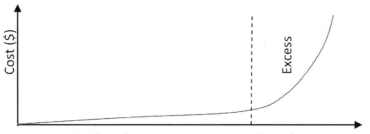

Attribute (e.g. size, weight, speed, etc.)

If an additional attribute only adds costs to the project, and this **attribute cannot be transferred to the price** that the client would pay, is probable that we are in a potential **excess** zone, where that attribute is unnecessary.

6.3 EXCESSIVE COMPLEXITY

There are hundreds of products and services that are so complex that they add very little value to the client. For example, let's think about the last remote control that we had in our home in order to simplify our life watching TV. Does it really simplify our lives?

If a newer remote control with 20 additional keys and functions comes out, would you throw out your current remote to buy that new one?

Neither would us! ☺

Why throw out the current remote that has dozens of buttons and functionalities, if we still don´t know how to use even 50% of all those functions?

Why abandon the latest Excel or Project software, if we still have not learned even 5% of them?

Case Korea – Excessive complexity

A company produced a car every two minutes. If by any reason production halted, that day was a huge headache for the company.

CEO: *How are we doing today with production speed?*

Technician: *Let's look at the dashboard, since we have it linked with the automation and control software, and the automatic reports from the management system, and..., and..., and..., and we will give you the report by tomorrow.*

CEO: *It is incredible what we've been able to do with all this science and technology. Many years ago, to get a progress report was much simpler. Have we entered into an excessive complexity road?*

From that moment, they started studying a simple tool where all company members could instantly know the production rhythm of the company.

They finally implemented in all of their production plants something very simple: a traffic light with three colors. Green indicates that everything is good; yellow means that a critical input is missing and that if it's not fixed, the machine will stop; and red indicates that the plant has stopped its production, something that everybody recognizes as a huge problem.

Not only that, but the red color triggers an alarm in relation to how to react upon. The person in charge of the production line has only 10 minutes to change the color red to yellow, or green. If he's not successful, his responsibility, and that's why he gets paid, is to inform the plant's general manager. The general manager has a maximum of two hours to try to fix the problem and if unsuccessful, his responsibility is to inform the company President.

By no means had the company abandoned the modern tools for the automation and control of the processes, with high quality progress reports, but they implemented a simple tool in parallel that everybody recognized instantly, regardless of their abilities and capabilities.

Conclusion: to implement technology by itself doesn't add value. Sometimes, simple methods can obtain better results.

Many companies forget that **adding more functionality, not necessarily adds more value**, from the client's point of view.

Going back to the remote control example, many people have bought very simple devices that have only three buttons: one to turn on/off, another for the volume, and the third to change the channel. What a marvelous technology! ☺

If we are planning the project schedule with Gantt chart software, where we have added thousands of activities, that during the project execution and control phase we will not be able to manage them, we surely have sinned in excess. A plan that will later not work on the execution and control, doesn't make sense.

A plan adds value only if it is used!

Excessive complexity on our projects will only get us:

- ✓ more costs,
- ✓ more errors,
- ✓ more misunderstandings, and
- ✓ more risks.

Many technological companies (e.g. Sony, HP, Canon, etc.) have discovered that a simple way to mitigate excessive complexity when developing a new product is to ask their technicians to explain the advantages of the new product in a **one-page executive summary**. The attributes not mentioned on that page are the potential excess candidates. If later on they have to speed-up development or reduce costs, what is not on that page are the first attributes to get eliminated.

LESSONS LEARNED

The excess of information, unnecessary attributes, or the excessive complexity, are examples of wastes that should not be added to the project.

Some tools to mitigate those wastes, to better know our client and the project scope are: iterative meetings between client and technicians, questionnaires to identify requirements, and budgets that are broken down by deliverable.

The excess and lack of information attempt against the project's profitability. We have to give our clients only what they asked for.

We should not keep adding additional attributes when the client doesn't pay for them anymore. Adding more technology or functionality doesn't mean more value for the client. Sometimes, simpler things add more value.

We should avoid excessive complexity. Otherwise, our projects will have: more costs, more errors, more misunderstandings, and more risks.

Finally, a plan is useful only if it will be used.

7 COMMANDMENT #2
HONOR DELIVERABLES
TO THE CLIENT

Do not honor with hatred the one you cannot honor with love.

FRIEDRICH HEBBEL. (1813-1863)

German poet

Every activity should have a deliverable and every deliverable should have a client. We must always think about our clients, whether internal or external, when conducting project activities.

7.1 LINK ACTIVITIES

In traditional project management , we are used to work logically with successor and predecessor activities. For instance, until Activity A is completed, we can't start with Activity B. In other words, until we have not received deliverable A, we will not be able to work with B.

However, in many opportunities while waiting for deliverable A, without even participating in that activity, we suffer many delays and inconveniences with the development of B.

We could think that B is an internal client of A, in a way to improve efficiency in the management of those project deliverables, and try to link both activities for the benefit of the project.

With this small linkage between A and B we could avoid misunderstandings and accelerate the project's completion. Let's look at the following case to better comprehend this concept of linking activities and honoring deliverables to an internal client.

Case Peru – Internal Client

The Program Manager was waiting for deliverable A (cash flow and financial indicators for the infrastructure project) in order to start working with activity B (cash flow and financial indicators for the program).

PM: *When do you estimate you will finish with A?*

A: *On the date we agreed.*

Fulfilling to perfection Parkinson's Law (work expands so as to fill the time available for its completion), deliverable A was delivered the last available day that they had to send the report.

PM: *You made some errors, because you should have formulate road projects cash flow to 20 years, instead of 10 years like you did, and the social discount rate should be 12 %, instead of the 10% you used.*

A: *But nobody ever mentioned that before, we already finished the printed report and was delivered on time, and we already have been assigned to another project. We don't have any resources to make any changes to the final report at this time.*

The PM did not have any other choice than to work extra hours to fix those errors in order to advance with activity B. However, he could not avoid the delays to the project caused by those errors that he ended up fixing.

If the PM would have gone to the team A, a couple of days before the due date and offer some help to review the work, surely there would not have been any delays. On the contrary, by detecting those two minor errors, on an early phase were the team had not printed the final report, they would have very easily added 10 cells to the worksheet with a different discount rate to the one they were using.

Team A didn´t want to change his work just because they didn´t want to re-print the final report. If the PM were collaborated with them before the printing, no delays would have occurred.

Conclusion: The internal client must link himself with the members of his predecessor activities, if we want to mitigate risks and delays.

The three key concepts to linking activities and honoring deliverables to the client are:

1. The client gets involved early
2. There is a brief period of joint collaboration between client and the predecessor activity team
3. The client is the one who determines the end of its predecessor

Let's look at those three concepts with a sport analogy. In the world of track and field, one of the team races consist of four athletes running 100 meters each one with a baton in hand, which must be handed to the other teammate in order for her to run her 100 meters. The winning team is the one that takes its baton around the 400 meters the fastest.

> The client gets involved early: the one who's waiting for the baton is not on its playing field, instead, it has introduced itself to its teammate's playing field to receive the baton.

> Brief collaboration period: the one who delivers the baton doesn't release quickly, instead running jointly with its teammate until they reach its playing field, then he transfers the baton.

> The client determines the end of the task: whoever takes the baton is the one that ends the transaction and verifies that everything is good, not the athlete that delivered the baton.

7.2   PRELIMINARY PROTOTYPES

In those cases where we don't know the ideal result of the deliverable that the client expects to receive, instead of delivering the final product per the specifications on a contract or industry standard, it is better to work with preliminary prototypes with partial approvals. This way, the needs and requirements are re-defined in conjunction with the client.

Traditional Management

For example, a multinational company requested authorization from governmental health authorities to approve the launch of a new mass consumption product that they had finish. These approvals took several years.

Also, another international company, once it finished an airplane, it requested authorization to the Federal Aviation Administration to approve that product, which also took several years.

Agile management

Both of these companies, when they started working with preliminary prototypes and partial approvals with the authorities, they managed to lower down several months delays approvals in relation to the traditional management style.

When we think about our internal client and we involve them from the early project phases, the expected results are more favorable.

7.3   ANTICIPATE INFORMATION

Sometimes waiting for a definitive approval of a deliverable in order to move forward tends to add too many delays to projects. For example, big organisms on the public sector are plagued by bureaucratic approval processes, where documents must go through many internal divisions to receive the stamps of approval.

In these cases, anticipating deliverable information to the client or the approving authority could be a good practice, for the purpose of accelerating the approval cycles and decision making.

Traditional management

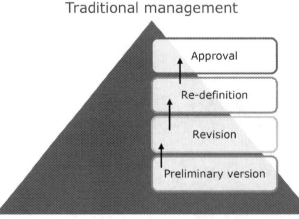

For example, in traditional management, the preliminary version is sent to the revision department. Then the document is sent to the re-definition department and once it gets to the approval department, it is sent once again to the requester to make corresponding changes. This is similar to the dairy model or the recurrent approval cycles that we discussed on previous chapters.

If possible, whoever starts the transaction could treat the approving authority like an internal client, sending the same document that's been waiting on the hallways of other bureaucratic departments that work with the "first come, first serve" scheme. This way, the client could give an anticipated feedback of the changes that it will require before the final report arrives to its department. With that preliminary feedback we could start working on the changes to advance process times.

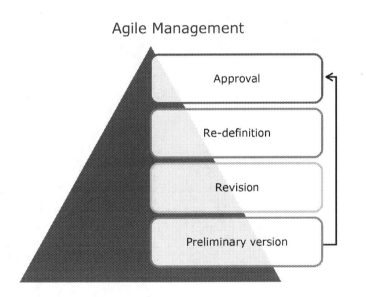

Agile Management

LESSONS LEARNED

A client is not only the user of a good and service, or the sponsor of a project. We should also consider as a client the members of our internal team and the external approving entities.

We have to link the predecessor and successor activities such that the internal client gets involved early in the process with the team that is working in the predecessor activity. We should also seek and foster a brief collaboration period between the team and the client.

The preliminary prototypes are usually very effective in involving the approval authorities in the formal project approval process.

Lastly, providing information ahead of time to the approval authority could be a good strategy to obtain preliminary feedback on the changes required on the project.

8 COMMANDMENT #3

YOU SHALL NOT WASTE TIME IN MEETINGS

I wasted time, and now doth time waste me.

WILLIAM SHAKESPEARE. (1564-1616)

British writer

In many companies, the meeting culture is so rooted that it looks like the only available time to add value is during the night or on weekends.

In this chapter we will see that this culture of eternal and inefficient meetings is a hindrance to projects and generates waste in the organization. But the most interesting thing is that we will develop some simple tools to comply with the third commandment: "you shall not waste time on meetings".

8.1   TYPE OF MEETINGS

As we saw on chapter 4, "Time batches", we should be clear in that **meetings, by themselves, do not add value** to the client. In general, most of the meetings are type 1 waste: necessary, but with no added value. Worst of all, most of the time dedicated to meetings falls into the category of type 2 waste or muda, which could be eliminated.

We should have in mind that meetings imply taking people out of their work place, which is truly where they really add value to the project.

Some polls mention that executives allocate an average of 30% of their time in meetings, which is equivalent to approximately 1.5 days weekly. But the amazing thing is that executives answer that half of the time spent on those meetings was unproductive.

This non-value added time is due, among other things, to the fact that:

- ✓ They waited for people to start the meeting,
- ✓ They had to wait until their relevant topic was discussed,
- ✓ They wasted too much time discussing irrelevant topics.

What about meetings you like the least?

Decisions were not made	18%
Participants unprepared	16%
Agenda was not followed	12%
Did not start on time	11%
Too long	11%
They were not well directed	11%
Not focused on the agenda	11%
Inadequate meeting minutes	7%
My participation was not necessary	4%
TOTAL	100%

Source: 3M

In general, in the project management world we tend to find two muda-causing types of meetings: coordination meetings and collaboration meetings.

Coordination meetings are those directed by the project manager, where team members are gathered to facilitate collaboration and communication among them.

On the other hand, **collaboration meetings** are those conducted by the project work team members to discuss any technical problem or to develop a market opportunity.

In both meeting types we commit similar bad time management sins. However, these are meetings with different underlying problems, which is why they will be treated separately on the following sections.

Case Mexico – The success of not meeting

A couple of years ago, we got to manage an investment project about distance learning courses. The distances between our workplace and Mexico, plus the great geographical dispersion between the different team members, made it really difficult to coordinate meetings where all stakeholders could participate.

When the project was nearing completion, we dedicated various days to plan the presentation format, including the main results of the job performed: diagnostic, alternatives, strategy, product, profitability, etc. But the hardest part was still missing; to find a date where all stakeholders could be present.

As we prepared the presentation, we decided to put lots of animations and recorded voices on the background, explaining in detail each slide. This will serve in order to send the presentation via email to the stakeholders, in case the meeting date kept being delayed.

Finally, we sent the dynamic presentation to evaluate the project. That way, we would leave the meeting to only discuss final details. The response to the presentation was spectacular. They could not believe that in only twenty minutes, the time that the presentation lasted, and without moving from their desk, they perfectly understood the project.

The impact was so strong, that the meeting was not necessary. Better yet, in a few months, the project was in full execution and with profitability over the estimated mean.

Conclusion: There are times that a meeting's success is not doing it!

8.2   COORDINATION MEETINGS

Discussing technical problems in a coordination meeting is usually a mistake. This type of discussion should take place in a separate meeting and use the time on coordination meetings to evaluate topics like:

- Define who is about to start a project activity.
- Evaluate who is about to finish a project activity
- The material and human resources team members need to perform project activities without obstacles or interruptions.
- Facilitate the project's execution according to plan.

This type of meetings is done on a weekly basis in many organizations, with an average duration of one hour, in the best-case scenario.

As shown in the following figure, the farther we are from the day of the meeting, the lower the effort we put into preparing for it. For example, if the meeting was every Friday, on Mondays we would dedicate a small amount of time to work on the project and then on Thursday evenings we would work intensely on completing all pending project issues for that meeting.

This delay for the preparation of the topics for the meeting could be harmful, because you need to put an extra effort trying to remember topics covered days ago. In addition, this time between meetings could generate type 2 wastes, by wasting time at the beginning of the meeting introducing topics discussed the previous week.

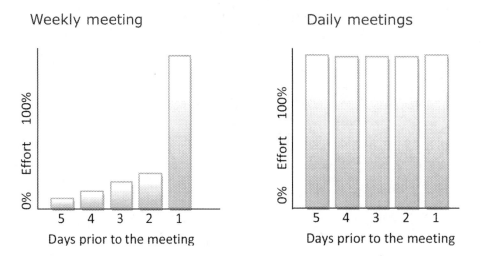

What we are suggesting is to change those weekly one-hour meetings by more frequent meetings, for example: **daily 10-minute meetings**. If you conduct a monthly meeting in your company, you could start by increasing the frequency to weekly meetings.

Coordination meetings should be very brief with much simpler topics, like for example:

- What value did you create yesterday?
- What are your plans for today?
- What do you need from the rest of the team to achieve your objectives?

Daily meetings force team members to maintain a constant effort to prepare them. At the same time, these frequent meetings will bring additional advantages, like the following:

- Facilitate resource re-allocation on real time.
- Prioritize those value-adding activities.
- Establish a clear work plan for each day.
- Keep team members emotionally committed.

You should not fall into the mistake of being too orthodox in the planning of coordination meetings, because sometimes is necessary to have these meetings due to specific urgent events. Although we said that these meetings should not be too spaced, their frequency should reflect the pressures of meeting project deadlines, costs, quality, and scope.

For these meetings to be effective, it is necessary for all interested parties to be present. However, you should not try to coordinate more than 15 people at the same time. If the project team is bigger than that, divide it in sub-groups to coordinate them separately.

Case South Africa - Meeting careless

It is customary to say that the key to the success of a good meeting is the good planning of the agenda and the good time management to adjust to the agenda.

That is necessary, but not enough. Any neglect during the meeting could ruin all the planning and time management. The facilitator for a work group's coordination meeting had finalized the details for the meeting's sound system prior to the meeting. While the room was filling with meeting participants, he took the opportunity to go to the restroom. When he returned to the podium to start his presentation, everybody could not stop laughing and everything was out of control.

What happened? Well, by careless, the facilitator had leaved his wireless microphone on in the restroom and everybody was listening the sounds made during his bathroom break.

Conclusion: It is good to break the ice at the start of a meeting. A good way is to make people laugh... but please, do not forget to turn the microphone off after sound check, if you pass by the restroom. ☺

8.3   COLLABORATION MEETINGS

While coordination meetings only require a revision of the project's status, in collaboration meetings you discuss the project's progress and technical problems in greater depth. Generally, these technical meetings are conducted with few participants.

The objective of these meetings is to share knowledge, choose between different alternatives, and resolve technical problems.

Like in coordination meetings, some organizations agree to have them on a weekly basis. As we show on the following figure, the more spaced are the meetings, the greater the risk of generating wastes or inefficiencies in the project.

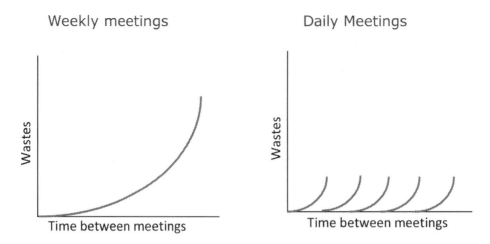

For example, if a team member discovers an error or problem during the week, it tends to keep that valuable information as a discussion topic for the next meeting. This time batch could cause great inefficiencies if the rest of the team keeps on working without knowing about the problem, because until they know about the error, all their work would have been in vain.

Also, the suggestion for resolving this problem is very simple: shorten the frequency of the meetings and to focus meetings on topics like:

- Who is the product's customer?
- What tangible product are we creating?
- How will the product affect our project's success?

Recommendations for collaboration meetings

1. Restrict the meeting to NO MORE than two hours.
2. Prepare topics in advance.
3. Have only one topic in the agenda, or several that are closely related.
4. Only invite people that need to be there, with punctuality... The rest are not welcome.
5. Respect the meeting's completion schedule to avoid Parkinson's Law: "work expands so as to fill the time available for its completion". In other words, the meeting will extend to all the available time if the schedule is not respected.

We recommend conducting collaboration meetings in a room where the project information is centralized. How much time is wasted looking for the necessary information? ... and finding the latest updated versions?

These types of inefficiencies need to be avoided, by building what is called a **project room**, and team members will ensure that only updated information is stored there. In those projects where the distance between team members prevents having a physical meeting room, a good alternative is to build a virtual project room on the Internet.

Case Spain - Leave footprints in your meetings

During a business trip in Europe, we had a collaboration meeting in a small city of Spain. In that opportunity, we were supposed to discuss the progress of a project about frozen gourmet products that will be part of the city's business incubator, which in turn is part of the business incubator network of the European Community. This was the third collaboration meeting between four team members to discuss some technical alternatives.

Start of the meeting, the conversation:

Mary: *Who was responsible of investigating the technical alternatives that the Asian countries are using?*

George: *Didn't we discuss that on our last meeting?*

Mary: *I was convinced that was decided on the previous meeting.*

Peter: *But I thought you were doing that.*

Then... "back to square one...".

What was the root cause of the problem? Not leaving minutes of the decisions taken on the previous meeting. That was exactly our mistake! We did not keep in mind that each individual selects and retains information differently. What for some may be very important, for others may be the least significant.

Conclusion: Always document a meeting's most important decisions in writing, including roles and responsibilities for each one involved. This way, you will create sort of a shared memory within the team with some tangible benefits, like:

- Decrease the need to constantly revise past decisions.

- Easily summarize old decisions and important topics.

- Increase confidence in that the decisions taken will be implemented with concrete actions.

LESSONS LEARNED

Meetings that are programmed with many invitees and with an endless agenda are part of a non-agile culture.

A project-oriented enterprise demands short and intense meetings, scheduled only when they are necessary.

Coordination meetings should only be made to facilitate the uninterrupted project's execution. While in collaboration meetings, only technical problems should be discussed.

Long and periodical meetings that are spaced, for example monthly or weekly are generally the cause of muda. Reducing the duration and frequency, for example, having daily ten-minute meetings, could eliminate this waste.

Lastly, there are times when not having a meeting is the key for a successful meeting.

9 COMMANDMENT #4

YOU SHALL NOT FORGET THE RISK ANALYSIS

Who searches for the truth...
runs the risk of finding it.

MANUEL VICENT (1936-?)
Spanish writer

If we want to accelerate project deadlines, having good risk identification, quantification, prioritization, and response plan, is fundamental.

9.1 RISK ANALYSIS

Risk is an uncertain event that, if it happens, will have a negative or positive effect on the project. Risks cannot be eliminated, but they can be managed.

Project risk management is a systematic process that identifies, analyzes, prioritizes and responds to the risks. According to the PMBOK® Guide, there are six risk management processes, which are the following:

1. **Planning**: is where you decide how to plan for risk management on the project activities.
2. **Identification**: it determines which risks could affect the project and their characteristics are documented.
3. **Qualitative analysis**: it evaluates the impact and probability of the identified risks, prioritizing them according to their potential impact on the project.
4. **Quantitative analysis**: it numerically analyzes the probability of each risk and its consequences over the project objectives.
5. **Risk response planning**: actions are developed to improve the opportunities and to reduce the threats to the project objectives.

6. **Monitoring and controlling**: monitoring of identified risks is performed, residual risks not previously identified are detected, and new risks are identified.

It is not the objective of this book to go into detail about the project's risk analysis. However, we will briefly explain how to perform a risk analysis with three basic steps:

- **Identify** risks in schedule, costs, scope, and quality.
- **Qualitative analysis** to estimate the possible impact, probability of occurrence, and probability of detection for each one of the identified risks.
- **Prioritization** of risks and decision-making.

9.2   RISK IDENTIFICATION

Interviewing specialized people is one of the most utilized techniques of the risk identification process.

Generally, the person responsible for the risk identification selects the appropriate individuals to interview, fills them in on the project, and asks them for their opinion about the risks on their project area.

With the interview process you can obtain information about the associate risk related to the scope, time, costs, and quality.

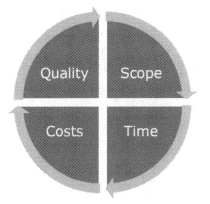

Interviews allow for the identification of the main project risks and are the starting point for the qualitative analysis.

The document that includes all possible project risks is not the only final result of the risk identification process. You will also identify the risk triggers. For example:

- A delay in one of the activities of the project's critical path can be the trigger to estimating a delay on the complete project.
- The effect of a tornado could be the trigger to estimating a price increase of agricultural products.

9.3   QUALITATIVE ANALYSIS AND PRIORITIZATION

Once risks are identified, it is necessary to classify them. You can prioritize risks with the qualitative analysis by defining the following for each one of them:

- The probability of occurrence.
- The magnitude of the impact on the project.
- The probability of detecting the risk event.

With the traditional risk management approach, only the probability of occurrence and the impact are considered. However, we have introduced a third variable to the risk analysis: the probability of detection.

For example, it is not the same to be driving your car and break your engine because you are out of oil; to having a red light on your dashboard that indicates "you are about to be without oil". When there is the possibility of detecting a risk event you have a better chance of avoiding a problem, than when there is no possibility of detection whatsoever.

If a hurricane is identified as a possible risk, you could ask the experts about the probability of a hurricane passing through the project's location, how bad would the impact be on the project (in time, costs, scope, quality), and what is the probability of detecting it with some anticipation.

In the qualitative risk analysis, the response to each one of these unknowns could be: very high, high, medium, low, and very low. But you could select a more ample scale, like 1 to 10, or a more simple scale: high, medium, and low. With these definitions for probability of occurrence, impact, and probability of detection, we can develop a risk matrix like the one shown next.

Probability	Impact	Detection	Priority
High	High	Low	HIGH
...	...	...	
Medium	Medium	Medium	MEDIUM
...	...	...	
Low	Low	High	LOW

We could categorize risks with high, medium, or low priority. This classification is subjective and it varies for each particular project.

The worst risk would be the one with a high probability of occurrence, high impact on the project, and a low probability of detection. On the other hand, the least significant risk would be the one with a low probability of occurrence, low impact, and a high probability of detection.

We could also quantify the risk by assigning some ordinal valuation. For example, we could assign a score of 1, 2, and 3. Where 1 means not important and 3 means very important. Then, those values are multiplied and a qualitative score is calculated for each identified risk.

Probability	Impact	Detection	Score	Priority
High = 3	High = 3	Low = 3	27	HIGH
...	...	...		
Medium = 2	Medium = 2	Medium = 2	8	MEDIUM
...	...	...		
Low = 1	Low = 1	High = 1	1	LOW

As we can observe, based on this scale, the most significant risk has a score of 27 and the least important has a score of 1. Using these values, we could classify the risks or they could be grouped in risk categories. For example:

- Score 1 to 3: low priority risks.
- Score 4 to 9: medium priority risks.
- Score 10 to 27: high priority risks.

It is worth clarifying that this is only an example of how to use the methodology; the ordinal values and the risk categories will vary for each particular project.

Although it is true that these risk categories are subjective, they are very useful to classify risks. Once classified, they can be prioritized and see which one of them require more analysis and which ones are not relevant and do not need more analysis.

There is no doubt that this subjective tool is not exactly precise. However, it tends to be very useful and practical to start with a simple risk analysis. Afterwards, those high priority risks should be examined with a more exhaustive analysis.

📖 Exercise 7 – Qualitative risk analysis

Romina Enrik, General Manager for an international company, is reviewing the final design for a telecommunications project with her work team.

<u>Romina</u>: *Gentlemen, I suggest we do not waste more time on these types of design revisions and put into practice Paul Leido's 4th Commandment: "perform a risk analysis". Why don't we leave the congratulations for our design for the bar? Today we could leave two hours early to celebrate that our client approved our project plan. Let's take advantage of this meeting to perform a qualitative risk analysis so we can prioritize the possible risks that we could face on the execution phase.*

The original project schedule can be affected by delays in customs due to possible strikes that have been announced by the port authority workers. In case of a strike, the schedule will suffer a delay of a few days, which represents a low impact to the project. The probability of occurrence for this risk event is estimated to be high. Meanwhile, the probability of detecting the strike a few days earlier is medium.

On the other hand, the technical people have detected that adverse weather factors could occur. In case of unfavorable weather, there will be a high impact on the project's schedule. There is a high probability of bad weather during the season when the project will take place. The probability of detecting the bad weather with anticipation is low.

Last, it can be expected that some workers could get sick during the project's implementation. If this happens, which has a medium probability, the project's schedule could be moderately delayed. The probability of detecting this risk event with anticipation is low.

Which priority would you give to each identified project risk?

✋ Take 10 minutes to answer before moving on with the reading.

& Answers - Exercise 7

Working with a qualitative scale of 1 (good) to 3 (bad), we put the risk scores and the priority for each risk on the following table.

	Impact	Probability	Detection	Score	Priority
Strike	1	3	2	6	3rd
Weather	3	3	3	27	1st
Sickness	2	2	3	12	2nd

Once the most important risk is identified, in this case the weather, it is necessary to develop a response plan for that risk. For example, if retaining walls or evacuation plans are developed, once the weather event happens the impact will not be as high. Meanwhile, if the project start date is changed, they could work during a season of lower weather risk, so the probability of bad weather will not be as high. Last, if a specialized meteorological service is acquired, they could have early warning systems that would alert them when the bad weather is coming, and they would be better prepared for that negative event.

Recommendations for risk analysis meetings

1. Restrict the meeting to no more than half day. If necessary, divide the project into smaller parts to be discussed separately.
2. Only invite the right people that know about possible risks.
3. Prioritize quality over the quantity of meeting invitees.
4. Perform a brainstorm session with the members of the meeting to identify possible risks.
5. Do not spend more than thirty minutes discussing each one of the potential risks identified.
6. Quantify in a qualitative way each one of the identified risks, based on their probability of occurrence, impact, and probability of detection.
7. Classify the quantified risks in bigger categories. For example: high, medium, and low priority.
8. Concentrate in further analyzing those risks with high priority, and develop response plans for them.

LESSONS LEARNED

Performing a risk analysis before starting with the project execution is being proactive by mitigating future problems, which will help you get a more agile and efficient project.

It is clear that risks cannot be eliminated. However, we can always manage them through a good planning, identification, qualitative analysis, quantitative analysis, response planning, monitoring, and controlling.

With the qualitative risk analysis you can detect the most significant risks that could affect the project costs, quality, and deadlines, with the purpose of prioritizing and implementing response plans to those risks, to mitigate them.

*"If you have a dream
and believe in it...*

*you run the risk to
make it happen"*

Walt Disney

10 COMMANDMENT #5

YOU SHALL TAKE AWAY TRADITIONAL METHODS

Assist a man in raising a burden, but do not assist him in laying it down.

PYTHAGORAS OF SAMOS (582 AC-497 AC)
Greek philosopher and mathematician

We will reflect upon those traditional inefficient processes that are impregnated in some organizations, and yet we do not change, convinced that they are a necessary evil.

10.1 AVERSION TO CHANGE

Throughout the years, enterprises have built bureaucratic project management processes that, in some cases, no longer apply to the modern times we are living. However, since these processes are so deep rooted within the company and work "well", nobody has the intention of changing them. As you may have observed, the word "well" is in quotes. That is because we could improve these outdated processes in order to achieve an agile project and avoid unnecessary conflicts.

However, why nobody cares to change these traditional processes for something better?

Next, we will tell a story to respond to that question.

People don´t mind change...

they just don´t want to be changed.

Case Germany – The three cats experiment

A few scientists decided to make an experiment. They locked three cats in a room and placed a glass of milk in a corner.

Quickly, one of the cats wanted to drink the milk and the scientists sprayed the three cats with cold water.

Another cat tried to drink the milk and they were sprayed again with cold water.

After a few wet tries, the cats, which are not dumb, learned the relation between trying to drink the milk and the cold water. Hence, none of them tried it again.

The scientists took one of the cats out of the room and brought in a new cat. The new cat immediately tried to drink the milk, but the other two cats beat the heck out of it, because they wanted no part of the cold water. The new cat quickly learned the lesson: *"I'm not going there again, or I'll get beat up"*, he thought.

Then they took out another one of the old cats and brought in a new one. This new cat also got beat up when he tried to drink the milk.

Finally, the scientists exchanged the third of the old cats for a new one, which also got beat up when he tried to get the milk.

There were none of the original cats left in the room. However, the cats did not want to get close to the milk for fear of retaliation from the others.

The scientists disconnected the water hose and left. Years passed and none of the cats ever approached the milk. Even if one of them did, nothing would have happened, but they did not do it because the traditional process said: *"that is not allowed!"*

Conclusion: The problem with companies that do not want to change their customary project management processes, is that many times these are only justified by a tradition.

As inferred from the previous story, some organizations have not asked themselves if those historical processes, which could have been very useful in the past, are still valuable in today's world.

10.2 THE FROZEN STAGES

A problem that some traditional processes usually have is that the stages of a project are too far or separate from each other. The excuse for not having parallel activities is that it would increase the risk of the project. However, in many instances the underlying reason is the objection to change and to stay rooted on traditional processes.

For example, on a house building project a traditionalist builder would prefer to wait until the client has defined with precision all formal specifications in order to start the construction phase. This way, the builder prevents the risk of starting with something that at some point does not meet customer specifications. Then, a dissatisfied client could request changes to what has been done already and this involves many headaches and monetary consequences.

However, these types of risks could be avoided with the implementation of the modern concept of working with frozen stages. This approach can work different stages in parallel without increasing the project risks and shortening its duration of completion.

Following with the house building example, the client may define some general preliminary specifications or drawings for the structural work. These preliminary data will be enough for the builder to lay the foundation of the structure. Then, once work is underway, the client may define in detail the type and design of the roof for the structure. Finally, with the structural work well advanced, the client could define the preferences and details regarding terminations for the interior of the structure. This frozen stages work approach, can shorten the project duration without major risks, as shown in the chart below.

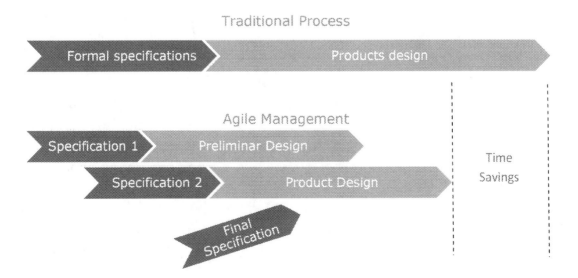

10.3 THE FUNNEL OF THE FROZEN STAGES

The frozen stages approach can be conceptualized as a funnel where as a project progresses and decisions are taken, it becomes extremely difficult and costly to go back.

At the top of this funnel the project definition is quite diffused, so that it could be defined as "anything goes". Once this preliminary and diffused stage is passed, the customer and the contractor should agree on a conceptual design for the work to be done. After this stage they could define a preliminary prototype before reaching a definite product.

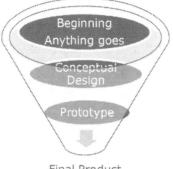

Final Product

One of the great advantages of working with this frozen stages approach, or stages that had been agreed by all parties, is that it avoids typical problems that are common for traditional processes. Generally, the client requests a final product and even though we think all specifications had been well defined in the contract, reality is that specifications are quite diffused at the beginning of any project. Usually, the contractor carefully follows all specifications detailed in the contract, but despite this, the client ends dissatisfied with the final product and, therefore, with the contractor.

By defining frozen stages between the parties, the customer agrees to the decisions taken as the project progresses. With these pre-agreed decisions, the client becomes aware of how expensive or impossible would be to go back or change a decision. This approach also offers some flexibility to the parties in order to incorporate new findings or needed strategic changes, which often occur while a project progresses.

This approach is not perfect, but if any small portion of a typical change in the life of a project could be anticipated and captured within each frozen stage, then a considerable amount of money and time could be saved.

Case Greece - Webpages Design

The company Webmaker suffered of constant and countless loss of time and money because of their indecisive customers who changed their minds about the webpage design that had already been finalized and delivered according to budget and work plan. This happened because customers had no clear idea of what their needs were at the beginning of the project and it was not until they got the finalized product when these needs were finally defined. Then, Webmaker decided to change the way they work with their clients, by defining the following frozen stages:

1st meeting – Show various working webpages to the costumer and determine if any of them satisfies the requirements described in the contract.

2nd meeting – Define the programming language to be used: html, flash, etc.

3rd meeting – Show the client three preliminary prototypes to choose from.

4th meeting – Deliver the final product of the webpage.

With this new system of work, Webmaker considerably improved its relationship with clients and started saving resources and time. Meanwhile, customers began to commit from the beginning of the project and realized that once they took any decision, any future change would be at their expense. It also happened in some cases that customers did not take decisions at the beginning because they were unsure, which caused the project to be on stand-by until a decision was taken. In these cases, customers understood that only them were responsible for any delay in the delivery of the final product in accordance to the original contract.

Conclusion: Working with a frozen stages approach helps clients to understand that any change of requirements in relation to a previously approved stage will delay the project and make it more expensive.

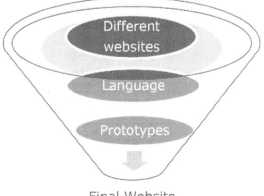

Final Website

10.4 SPEED OF THE FROZEN STAGES PROCESS

When implementing the frozen stage scheme a trade-off appears between:

- To accelerate the process, to quickly get a limited final product.
- To delay the process, to obtain a final product that evaluates several alternatives for a longer term in its execution.

As seen in the chart below, if a process is shortened too much and a cattle concept is defined on the diffused extreme of the funnel, a poultry concept could not be obtained as the final product.

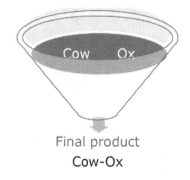

Final product
Cow-Ox

Accelerating the process may cause us to analyze just a few alternatives, for example the cattle project: cow and ox. Therefore, the final result would only be a cattle project: cow and/or ox, leaving aside other possible alternatives such as a poultry project.

On the other hand, if you delay a process, a larger amount of alternatives can be evaluated and the concept of the final product can be improved. For example, the following graph shows that on the initial end of the *anything goes*, you can weight upon alternatives such as: cow, tiger, chicken and horse.

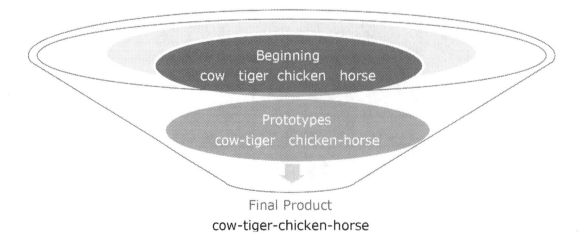

Final Product
cow-tiger-chicken-horse

As the process advances, preliminary prototypes could be outlined such as cow-tiger and horse-chicken. Imagine what it would be to have access to the biotechnology revolution and be able to take home a horse that lay eggs, give milk, and at the same time takes care of your home as a tiger.

¿How far we are from these things?

Case Italy – Online Shirts

The company *Shirties* lost a lot of money because of the constant changes of the fashion industry. It happened more than once that when the company was done with the process of making a shirt, which design was decided as a result of a market research, the fashion it suddenly changed. This adversely impacted the company, who was left with a large stock of shirts and was unable to sell even at discount prices.

When *Shirties* was on the verge of bankruptcy, it decided to change its traditional production and marketing approaches. It began selling shirts only online, but with a peculiarity: the clients were able to design their shirts according to their needs and taste. The company produced all the separate parts of a shirt with a large variety of fabrics, collars, buttons, pockets and cuffs. The customers were the ones who put together the parts that they liked the most. This online alternative allowed the customers to have a larger amount of possible combinations than any other traditional company.

This way *Shirties* was able to keep open the funnel of alternatives to choose from for all the customers until the final moment when payment was finalized via Internet. Materials used in the manufacture of these shirts that got out of fashion were easily placed individually to different wholesaler manufacturers and usually used for items other than shirts.

The success of *Shirties* was so great that major European companies implemented this same marketing system.

Conclusion: To keep the funnel open as much time as possible in order to offer customers a large selection alternatives, is usually of competitive advantage.

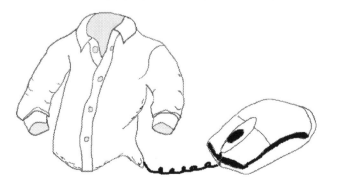

10.5 THE BLURRY CUSTOMER NEEDS

The most difficult part of the frozen stages process is to understand the blurry needs of a customer, in order to prevent future changes to an advanced project. There are some tools to deal with this situation, for example:

- **Iterative feedback** between designers and customers. If designers and technicians do not have fluid contact with the customer, then the project will fall in a risk of ending with a product made by engineers for the limited use of engineers.

- **Preliminary prototypes** built based on trial and error. Before taking the final product to the market, a preliminary test could be launched to assess the level of acceptance according to costumers. After getting feedback from clients, the prototype is improved for another test. This process of trial and error can shape a final product in a way that is ready for large scale production.

- **Involve senior management** in the project. In some projects the team gets isolated during the product development phase from both, the client and senior management. It then presents a final product that does not satisfy management and is subject to constant changes before presenting it to the client. Just as it is suggested an iterative feedback between the designer and the client, it is important to also get feedback from the designer and management while the project progresses.

- **Pseudo clients**. This method consists in converting technicians and designers in pseudo customers. In other words, designers make and use the product under development in the same way that the consumer would. The following case shows two examples of this tool.

Case Japan - Pseudo clients

When Nissan wanted to introduce its car models to the European market and before making any adjustments in their vehicles, it sent fifty technicians to live and operate the cars throughout Europe for six months.

On the other hand, when Matsushita created a small domestic oven to make bread and sales of that product were disastrous, it sent the oven designers to work as master bakers for three months in a traditional bakery.

Both Japanese companies achieved successful products once they applied the pseudo clients' technique.

Nissan developed special models for the European market, after a life experience that revealed the real needs of that market.

Meanwhile, Matsushita modified its original oven based on the experience of the engineers-bakers, and its product became a commercial success because the bread was an edible produce.

Conclusion: if you want a successful project, developers should put themselves in the customer's shoes.

10.6 LIFTING TRADITIONAL PROCESSES

We can extend the concept of lifting traditional stages to eliminate traditional processes. To explain this concept we will present the airlines' case.

Traditional processes of major international airlines and their vision of growth are based on using large hub airports and large-capacity aircrafts. These generate savings which maintain low operating costs and a low margin on the tickets' price. This is the concept of success that is steeped in these airlines, and their strategies are based on it.

But has anyone asked passengers for their opinion?

When conducting satisfaction surveys, passengers always point out that their main needs are:

- Security
- Reasonable price
- Door-to-door

Apparently, airlines have forgotten the passengers' need of door-to-door. This means that passengers would be willing to pay more if an airline offers to flight directly from the point of origin to destination.

The concept of large hubs and large aircrafts is totally against the door-to-door need. The following case shows one of many examples for this problem, which arises by continuing to implement and expand a traditional process.

Case Ecuador – How to travel from Quito to Mendoza

Thousands of frequent flyers who live in small towns are trapped in the traditional processes of the huge airlines.

A few years ago, and after a seminar in Quito (Ecuador), we have to travel to Mendoza (Argentina). We were lucky to find space in a point-to-point connection in order to get fast to our final destination. We left the hotel three hours before our flight and got to the airport two and a half hours prior to the flight departure time. This was a risky move because the trend is to be at the ticket counter three hours before an international flight and avoid a *"we are sorry, but we cancelled your ticket because you were not present on time"*.

When we arrived at the airport we made the first line where the officer only forgot to ask us about our blood type. Then we faced a second lengthy line to complete the check-in process for the flight, even though an hour was not that long when compared to traditional lines found in large hubs. The third line was to pay the exit taxes, but twenty minutes did not seem to be that bad either. Why not paying that tax at the check-in counter?

These lines were followed by two short but interesting lines: one person checked that the exit taxes paid were real and then another officer checked that our exit taxes were already verified. The sixth line was for immigration control and the seventh line for checking the hand baggage. Luckily we were on the final stretch, so after an eight line and a long wait, we got on the plane. The flight made a stop in Guayaquil, were we only wait for forty five minutes. It set off to Lima where we wait for another two hours in order to change planes. Obviously, we also endured long lines for luggage checks, because great geniuses from large hubs' international security decided so. Fortunately, after all corresponding lines were done we boarded and left to Santiago de Chile without any common flight delay.

In Chile officers checked our luggage again. After the corresponding line and a few more hours of waiting we boarded our flight to Mendoza. We were also lucky that the fog was not a factor to cancel the flight, as it usually happens. Once we arrived to Mendoza we stood on the large line for migrations for forty five minutes and our luggage was checked for the fourth time. Then we have to add the waiting time in the baggage claim area, which was also checked before leaving.

The truth is that everything went great and we got to Mendoza in record time: eighteen hours and fourteen lines! This is unusual because normally a flight gets delayed or cancelled and the normal is an average of twenty two travel hours. And we better not tell the story when we flight from San Pedro Sula (Honduras) to Mendoza, when a record flight takes thirty hours, after many stops through all existing hubs in Latin America. Not to mention our last travel to Santo Domingo (Dominican Republic) where after two cancelled flights, the odyssey turn into a forty nine hours flight.

Conclusion: According to passengers, many traditional processes have no real significance and could be lifted or eliminated.

Is not time for airlines to exploit this market for those travelers who are willing to pay more for a door-to-door flight?

Of course, this will require the complete lifting of traditional processes associated with major airport hubs and large aircrafts. The new concept should be base in processes that involve efficient small airports, take care of security with the minimum necessary controls, and that use small planes for direct flights between two small cities.

Perhaps this idea sounds idealistic and too distant at this moment, but if the traditional model continues to develop, not even low-cost alternative fuels will allow airlines to meet the door-to-door customer need.

Other alternatives to obtain the point-to-point benefit are trains or buses. However, some companies are copying the bureaucratic airport model, just because they do it, while forgetting the needs of the customers. If you do not believe me, take a tour to the modern bus terminal in Neuquen (Argentina) where the baggage handling and claim process has been copied from the airport model and it is done by using conveyor belts. It seems that they forgot that in the past the passengers could get to the bus five minutes before departure and it took them five minutes to get off the bus with their luggage included. This process has been changed for a pre-boarding time of thirty minutes and a luggage claim waiting time of another thirty minutes. Obviously, including the exit tax that corresponds in order to manage all of this!

If traditional processes cannot be eliminated, then at least, we should try **NOT to emulate those processes that neglect the customers' needs.**

LESSONS LEARNED

If your company is steeped in inefficient and traditional processes, ask yourself why not change them. If your answer is "*because tradition does not allow it*" then you should try to lift those processes. You may discover that this aversion to change, common in many organizations, is not hard to eradicate.

On the other hand, it is extremely important to get the client involved in the progress of the project. The frozen stages scheme is a very useful approach to accomplish this because project progress is defined cooperatively with the customer.

The hardest part of this scheme is to understand the blurry customer needs during the initial stages of a project. The following tools can be used in this case:

- Iterative Feedback between technical team and client.
- Analyze preliminary prototypes.
- Get senior manage involved early on any process.
- Place developers in the customer's shoes (pseudo clients).

11 COMMANDMENT #6
YOU SHALL COVET VISUAL METHODS

A man doesn't look at the sky just because it's in his sight.

JEAN-BAPTISTE DE MONET (1744-1829)
French Biologist

This commandment will analyze the importance of working with visual tools, instead of long text documents.

📖 Exercise 8 – Visual signals

Chapa Demo, project manager, has very few weeks for his team to finish a project. A key team member gets sick and it is urgent to hire a replacement in order to meet the project deadline. The approval for this replacement depends on the functional manager who is Chapa's boss.

Chapa: I have called several employees of the company and no one is available to come to work! I also sent several emails to my boss for help, but I have not received an answer. I went to the human resources department and requested an urgent hire of a trained person, or to reassign personnel from other areas to this project in order to save it, but none of them seem to be worried.

Several weeks later, this issue is addressed in a project progress meeting but the deadline is due. There is almost nothing that can be done in order to remedy the situation. Lost time could not be recovered, the project was delayed and the customer will be very unhappy.

Unfortunately many projects fail in fulfilling their objectives because of circumstances beyond the control of the project team. Managers are very good at solving problems, but it is not easy to find executives who make decisions in a timely manner that support their teams, so that potential problems are proactively mitigated.

How could this situation be mitigated in future projects? Can you think of a graphical method that can help? 🖐 5 minutes

📖 Answer - Exercise 8

Business managers are overwhelmed with urgent problems that they must address. When Chapa went to his boss to discuss his problem, probably he was told "*we will look into it*" as to test whether it was really important or not.

If we help managers by telling them only the information that is really important and highlighting the priorities, many projects may have more chances of success. However, communicating a project deviation through a spoken conversation, as Chapa did, is usually less effective than when communicating through visual graphics. For example:

- Mark in red those activities that are delayed and the new estimated end date due to the problem.
- Plot the total amount to be paid in fines due to the delay of an activity because of lack of human resources.
- Communicate through a histogram the over-allocation or lack of resources.
- Place traffic lights with colors showing the progress of the project.

Now we will develop several tips that will be useful when graphically communicating the progress of a project.

11.1 VISUAL METHODS

More than once you have heard the phrase "***a picture is worth a thousand words***". There is nothing more truly than this statement and that is what the commandment for this chapter is based on.

Written documents have the benefit of being very flexible, but they are generally inefficient. They fail by being full of too many words that could have been avoided. All of these words could have been replaced with more efficient tools using: colors, shapes, icons, charts, prototypes, etc.

There is nothing new on using visual methods, but it seems like humans have bureaucratized simple things with endless texts. Just think how centuries ago the Greeks and Romans conveyed flags as signals to delineate their tactics of war on the battlefield.

What do the following pictures mean?

Right! It does not matter if you speak Japanese or not, these pictures mean "trash" and common sense tell us that if it is in front of a PC, then everything we throw in it we will not use it again. This was the graphic concept that Apple Macintosh established for the first time as part of its operating system. This simple graphic avoided the need of writing long manuals to explain the meaning of these pictures.

11.1.1 Colors

Colors are a powerful tool that is used in conjunction with pictures.

What does the red color represent on the following Gantt chart?

Start	◇	
Prepare land		
Buy land	▮▮	
Smooth terrain	▮	
Plantation		
Plant olives	▮▮	30d
Plant vines	▮▮▮	
Plant plumbs	▮	40d
Install irrigation		
Import inputs	▮	
Install hoses	▮	
Install pumps	▮	10d
End	◇	

If you are an expert in project management and MS Project, there is no doubt that your answer was: the activities in red are critical. A critical activity is one that if it gets delayed, it delays the whole project. While activities in blue are those with slack. The days of slack for those activities represent the number of days this activity can be delayed without affecting the estimated completion date for the project.

Now, if this is the first time that you see a Gantt chart, surely your common sense led you to think that red means danger and blue means ok. Both, experts and novices came to the same conclusion.

The chart below shows a resources histogram. In this case the color red represents that the resource have been over-allocated. For example, it is most likely that Charlie won't be able to complete all the tasks he has been assigned with on the date of the over-allocation.

This can be easily explain because Charlie has only one head and two arms, and the day twenty four hours. Even though his boss thinks otherwise! ☺

Charlie	Jan	Feb	Mar	Apr	May	Jun
Over-allocated						
Allocated						
Resources allocated:		1	2	2	1	

11.1.2 Pictures

Another tool that speaks for itself are pictures.

In one of the latest trainings a participant asked: *"How is the Project Management congress in your city?"*

The answer was simple: *"look at a couple of outdoor pictures of the project teams on the mountains and wineries".*

After looking at a couple of pictures, the interested person answered: *"that is great, enough, I do not need to read all the content of the program!"* ☺

11.1.3 Figures

Our company of project consulting services, +C, has implemented a policy regarding the submission of written reports: anything that can be said in a **table format and/or graphics, does not need to be written**.

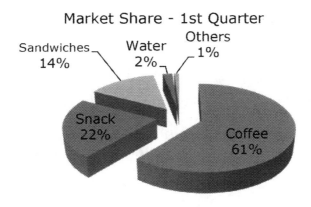

What sense does it have to present this graphic in a report and also write:

> *"As you can see, the market share in the first quarter is telling us that in the first place, coffee accounted for sixty-one percent of total sales, while in second place, snacks products had a twenty two percent of the market, in third place it can be observed the sandwiches with fourteen percent of the market, then water with two percent, and finally the services with a two percent stake."*

To write all of that would be wasting seventy words, spend too much time in writing, and it would also be against the lean and agile philosophies. Also, when the time comes to update the report, it is much more efficient to change the chart or table than to change everything that was written before.

Finally, those who write project reports know that even the most expert will usually update all graphics and will leave some text outdated. Why add unnecessary risks when writing texts?

11.1.4 Symbols

There are some companies who are using symbols to rapidly detect the status of their projects. For example, the international consulting firm Bain, who specializes in strategies, introduces to organizations a culture of symbols that all employees must understand and use on their project reports.

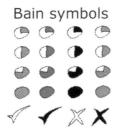

11.1.5 Prototypes

Another excellent visual tool used to present a project is through prototypes. This tool is commonly used by architects and engineers for building projects, where preliminary models are shown to costumers.

These prototypes can be made with three-dimensional simulation software, where the virtual experience of knowing the future project exceeds any written document.

Prototype   Real

11.2 VISUAL STATUS OF EXCEPTIONS

The information theory provides a powerful message: **"the value of information is not defined by similarities but differences".**

What do you remember from this morning travel to work?

If you remember nothing, is not for lack of memory, but because nothing extraordinary happened on your journey to work. Certainly, your memories are not everyday things like a collision, a protest, a new billboard, etc.

In the world of projects we should add value to management by reporting only those extraordinary events or project deviations. To do so, the company could develop a visual tool for exceptions.

We should help managers and simplify their decision making process by informing them about extraordinary events only. Going back to the Chapa exercise, it is not that executives do not listen or understand the problem, but that in their day-to-day lives they are constantly creating new businesses and firefighting. It is common for an executive to listen to many problems, so when another one comes, he acts like is made of Teflon. Much more when he finally discovers that most of those problems were not really a priority.

To improve the communication between the project manager and senior management a visual status of exceptions could be used, such as the charts shown below.

In the following table, the project leader reports on the progress of the project and its impact on cost, schedule and quality. Horizontal arrows represent normal, upward arrows mean very well, and downward arrows represent problems. These problems can be cost overruns, delays or poor quality of deliverables.

Task	Responsible	Cost	Schedule	Quality
Product design	J. Perez	↓	↓	↓
Packing design	M. Ruiz	↔	↔	↔
Production plan	F. Mir	↑	↑	↑
Select distributor	P. Pipe	↓	↔	↑

This type of reports can be sent periodically to the manager. With this simple visual outline, the manager can be in a better position to act on priority issues, and to respond to the project leader needs.

The following is similar to the previous approach, to evaluate the progress of a project portfolio by communicating the information using a visual status of exceptions.

Project	Responsible	Next deliverables	Status
A	Caroline P.	Preliminary demos	↓
B	Peter B.	Approve final test	↔
C	George S.	Pack to send	↑
D	Angela B.	Initial meeting of project	↔
E	Paul R.	Revision of design	↑
F	John A.	Sign contract with client	↓

Typically, an image is more efficient than several text documents. Working with a visual status of exceptions is very useful in helping management to differentiate the priorities of the project. This improves the decision making process, not only in favor of the project, but also in favor of the team.

LESSONS LEARNED

To write long texts stating the status of our project is inefficient. Instead, we should use graphic methods that will definitely bring more attention: **colors**, pictures, symbols, tables, prototypes, etc.

For senior management to care about deviations in a project, it is important to communicate the exceptions, instead of the similarities.

If we could implement a visual status of exceptions, it would be very useful in order to identify priorities and be proactive while eradicating the problems affecting the project.

12 COMMANDMENT #7

YOU SHALL NOT KILL STANDARD METHODS

Planning: worry about finding the best method to achieve an accidental result.

AMBROSE BIERCE (1842-1914)

American writer

This commandment means that if your company is already implementing efficient tools for project management, you should not try to change everything in order to be innovative. Make only the necessary innovations based on the lean-agile culture that you worked so hard to develop.

12.1 DO NOT REINVENT THE WHEEL

Why do major fast food restaurant chains
use recipes to make their hamburgers?

Those burgers could be made and eat without using any recipe. However, these old recipes allow other cooks to make exactly the same **without much effort** and it also helps the business model of these companies continue to grow around the world.

Without these recipes, this fast food chain would risk the quality of their food by having a large and unwanted variability. These scattered grades of quality would happen even if the company counts with the top chefs in the world to make simple burgers.

This example should not be very different in the world of projects. If a company has established efficient methods for repetitive activities of their projects ...

What is the need for reinventing the wheel?

Why not take full advantage of these successful methods, like paying the costs of the learning curve, and leave creativity for more important things?

There were some companies who had a *"we were 100% creative"* slogan who lost several million dollars and went bankrupt. To avoid this type of failure it is recommended **to use standard processes** already proven successful, for those activities that the project may require. This would be the case for processes for requesting a purchase order or loading a database.

Some work rules can also help define a culture of work and efficient standard processes, such as:

- Let no one be late to meetings,
- Prohibition of giving verbal instructions about project progress,
- Do not limit to a single budget, among others.

Based on these standard methods, it is necessary to keep improving the processes, as specified by the fifth lean principle. This will allow to keep improving the *recipe* without having to start all over again every time a new project is started.

A **standard method** is a recipe that allows any project team member to perform a task with the skill of an expert without the need of reinventing the wheel.

12.2 THE PMBOK® GUIDE

One of the main services offered by the Project Management Institute (PMI)[6] is the development of *standards* for the practice of project management around the world. For example, the Project Management Body of Knowledge (PMBOK® Guide) is an internationally recognized standard which contains a series of processes for efficient management of projects. This book also includes a glossary of definitions, concepts and generally accepted terms in this profession.

The PMI® institution was founded in 1969 and its headquarters are located in Philadelphia, USA. Within the PMI® *objectives* we can mention:

- increase the scope and quality in project management
- encourage the use of project management for the benefit of businesses and the general public

The PMBOK® Guide has been honored by the American National Standard Institute and today is one of the most famous books for project management. It covers ten basic areas of knowledge that are presented in the figure below.

---

[6] PMBOK is a registered mark of the Project Management Institute, Inc.

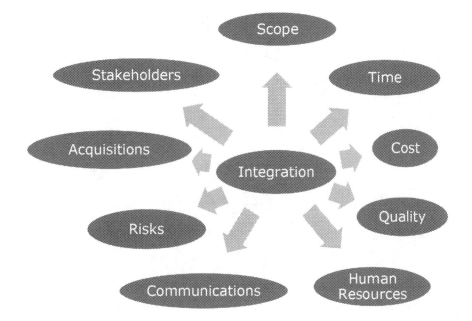

If there are already internationally accepted processes for the efficient management of projects, such as the PMBOK® Guide, then it is not justified to reinvent the wheel with new processes. This is what commandment 7 refers to, *"you shall not kill standards methods"*. [7]

We should further develop efficient management processes that are based on existing standards such as the PMBOK® Guide or the *Project Manager* book, and that does not mean lack of creativity.

Case Disney and Pixar - Processes versus creativity

Critics often say that standard processes are against creativity. But would not it be that thanks to efficient standardized processes the team can focus on planning creatively for a long term?

There is no doubt that Disney's animated films division had always had a lot of creativity. Their projects have been mainly based on craft films made of manual drawings ranging from Snow White and the Seven Dwarfs (1937) to The Lion King (1994). However, then Pixar became the leader of the "computer- animated movies" business.

---

[7]   PMBOK is a registered mark of the Project Management Institute, Inc.

Pixar is characterized by process automation and obeys four stages in the cycle of each project: development, preproduction, production and postproduction. Is Pixar less creative than Disney? Apparently that is not the case. In 1991 Disney made a strategic alliance with Pixar in order to incorporate computerized drawings technology and process automation in their new films, such as: Toy Story (1995), Finding Nemo (2003), The Incredibles (2004), and Monsters University (2013).

In 2003, the president of Pixar and founder of Apple, Steve Jobs, announced they were parting ways with Disney starting in 2006 because they never reached an agreement on intellectual property of the films. Disney stocks' value fell 4% with that announcement. This event may indicate that the market agrees with the creativity style of Pixar which is based on automated processes of project management. At the end, Disney acquired Pixar and paid with stocks from its company.

Conclusion: The case of Pixar is certainly an example of *standard methods* success associated with a highly creative activity. Standard methods do not kill creativity. They save costs and time, letting resources be used more efficiently to create value.

LESSONS LEARNED

If processes and traditional rules work well together...do not touch them! Leave creativity for more important things.

But... how? Didn't we say in commandment #5 to take away traditional methods?

It works like the Yin and the Yang, two opposed forces that complement each other and are present in all things. If something can be improved, improve it (commandment #5) and if a process works well, why touch it (commandment #7)?

You can be creative by following standard processes.

Finally, if you want to apply an efficient process management into your project, do not invent everything from scratch, and start with what is already available and has been proven on the market to be successful, such as the PMBOK® Guide.

13 COMMANDMENT #8

YOU SHALL NOT CREATE LONG WAITS

He who waits, despairs.

POPULAR PROVERB

The main message in this commandment is to think of customer satisfaction, internal or external, and to avoid processes that require long lines and unnecessary waits, as much as possible.

13.1 LINES AND WAITS

The project world we live in is full of lines and waits. Most of the public sectors deserve a special mention, which could be classified as the bureaucratic processes champions of lines and waits. These are many times originated in the management of physical documents and forms. As explained in previous chapters, this is one of the big faults to the flow of value which produces huge inefficiencies and delays in project management.

These waits are generally caused by the First-In-First-Out (FIFO) approach, just because some companies believe it is the most fair.

Believe it or not, this system is still applied not only by the public sector but also by the private sector. Like, for example, by some doctors, mechanics, computer technicians, hairdressers, restaurants, project managers, etc.

In the world of *lean-agile* projects, there is nothing more unfair than to create unnecessary waits or to not prioritize based on the value generated by each project.

The figure below shows the FIFO system.

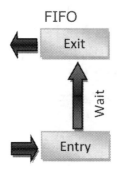

It is said that the FIFO scheme is a *necessary evil* that some organizations need to go through and, in the next chapters, we will learn some remedies for it.

13.2 RESERVATIONS SYSTEM

In all projects where the productive capacity of each resource is known and the arrival time of a need is well established, the First-In-First-Out (FIFO) scheme could be changed for a system of turns and reservations.

It is possible that the reader has ever suffered long hours of line and waits in a doctor's office. For that reason let's see if we can find a cure for this disease.

What is the need of a doctor to work with the FIFO scheme? Why some doctors do not respect the allocated time for an appointment? Is it that they believe their time is more valuable than ours? Or is it that they do not apply *lean-agile processes* for a better planning and time management?

Even in an area as complicated as health services, some companies that work through processes have shown that it is possible to move to a system of turns and reservations that benefits the client. This is shown in the figure below.

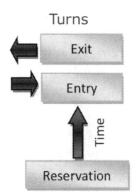

One example is the Zaldívar Institute, who has been internationally recognized for refractory eye surgery, has also been certified by ISO 9001 quality standards and uses an efficient system of processes that ensure great customer service with a minimum of lines and waits. This clinic knows that based on their physical equipment and human resources, they can only perform a limited number of consultations and surgeries every day. Therefore, they grant reservations in advance in order to ensure that patients do not have to wait.

Obviously, the Institute works with a risk management system to allow free time to treat emergency cases without interfering with the normal operation of the reservations.

Another example that is common whenever lines and waits systems are used, is when managers are very busy and a report gets held for several days, or months, at a desk before being reviewed. Instead, the manager could assign a turn to review that report. That way the team member can keep improving the report until the time comes for it to be reviewed. It is not an easy task, but in our service company +C, it has been implemented without much pain. All that is needed is to **want it, plan it** and some **agile** thinking.

All of the FIFO examples mentioned in the section above (doctors, mechanics, technicians, hairdressers, restaurants, project managers, etc.) could very well change to a turns and reservations system in order to fulfill the commandment "you shall not create long waits".

Case Epcot – Lines and Waits

In 1986, I was young and went to visit the great amusement park Walt Disney World. I learned that for most of the rides on high-demand, like the space mountain, we had to do several hours of lines and waits. One amazing thing I noticed was the statistical system used, because once you stood in line you knew exactly how many hours and minutes will take you in order to enjoy the ride. In my youth, I was amazed at such precise statistics, not common to see in my small city.

However, many years later I wondered... if these statistics were so spectacular, why not give me a turn that says? *"Come back in two hours and forty five minutes for your turn to the ride"*. I could have used my precious time in other less popular rides, buying popcorn, coke or taking pictures with some Disney characters. Not only would I have been happier but would have spent several additional dollars at Disney. As of today, Disney World began applying lean-agile thinking and offers the customer the option to take a turn (fast-pass) to take rides.

On the other hand, airlines have also begun to gather statistics to see how long it takes a passenger from the starts of the line until assisted on the counter. Many airlines have found that it is necessary to continue promoting that passengers arrive at the airport three hours before their international flights.

How much more would it take these airlines to apply a more agile process with reservations and turns? Do we have to wait several years like in the case of Disney World? Is it really so hard to give us a turn that says *"come back in two hours and you will be served"*? We could use that precious time to read the newspaper while drinking a coffee, to buy gifts, check emails and social media networks, call a friend using Skype, or to take a nap.

Conclusion: If we want to add value to our projects, then it is extremely important and fair to replace the *FIFO* system for a *reservation* system.

13.3 ELECTRONIC FILES SYSTEM

Sometimes, the bureaucratic management of physical files causes the FIFO system. No one in the team wants to move to the next stage of the project until they see the signature on the physical form or file.

Some functional organizations have offices that appear to be independent of the rest of the team. It even makes it difficult for anyone to know in which office the file got stuck. Usually, the answer to this problem is: "it is a necessary evil in order to have better control over the organization."

> Does "bureaucracy of physical records" really mean to have more control?
> Why not improve control with more efficient tools?

A very good remedy for this necessary evil is to move from a physical file scheme to an electronic file process. This change won't allow losing control and will streamline processes, resulting in a large time reduction.

Case Nigeria – Electronic Files

The company Think S.A. specializes in the implementation of processes to move from a lines-and-waits system of managing physical records, to an efficient management of electronic records. For example, at the South Municipality they implemented an electronic record system to grant a business license.

Before this change, granting a license took at least thirty days and many internal processes were sequential. Due to the amount of bureaucratic processes in place, there were more than 170 communication channels in order to grant a license to a single business.

An organizational change was essential in order to launch an electronic records system. It was also important to encourage the employees so that they wanted to change the process and thus achieve a better quality of life (better results with less effort). Therefore, the methodology of work was to get everyone involved and define the problem (the tangle of processes). This encouraged them to come up with suggestions for solutions to the problem. At the end and by consensus, employees themselves elected to change the way they worked.

After four months into the implementation of this project in the municipality, the computerized processes were being done in parallel with greater control than in the starting situation. The process for granting a business license dropped to an average of five days with less than 35 channels of communication related to the new process. Not to mention the large cost savings in stationery and environmental care achieved with this agile process.

Conclusion : Implementing agile processes do not imply to neglect monitoring and control mechanisms. On the other hand, it often strengthens control by eliminating bureaucratic and inefficient processes.

LESSONS LEARNED

We need to try working with a system of reservations and turns instead of a FIFO model which ignores priorities.

For several projects it would be better if a process of electronic files is implemented instead of a physical sequential process.

To streamline organization processes does not mean to have less control.

14 COMMANDMENT #9

YOU SHALL NOT FORGET THE CRITICAL RESOURCES

Adversity awakens in our resources that, under favorable circumstances, would have been asleep
QUINTO HORACIO FLACO (65 AC-8 AC)
Latin Poet

Through this commandment we will expand the traditional approach of the critical path in order to include risk planning, especially of those risks that can delay your project.

📖 Exercise 9 – Risks on planning

Peter Littleluck, project manager of an energy company, had one of its worst days at work.

First, Martin Stuart tells him that he cannot complete the installation of the new generators on time and meet the deadline agreed with the client. Therefore, a natural gas refinery has no power to operate. The client, an oil company, will lose a million dollars per week because of this delay. Martin had not report any delay on the project schedule before, because this technical issue caught him off-guard.

The second bad news is that Marcel Led told Peter that the test plan is hampered by the lack of available engineers. Although the generators were already finished, they could not function because the tests are delayed. The additional delay is estimated in at least two weeks.

Mr. Littleluck is very angry...

<u>Peter</u>: *I cannot believe it! When we started this project I asked to be informed of all the critical needs and resources. You assured me that the test plan would be completed before the deadline and that this activity had several weeks of slack. For that reason I did not add this event to the critical path's "watch list". Now, an activity that had a significant slack is part of the critical path!*

What is the main cause for the delay on these activities? 🖐 10 minutes

📖 Answer - Exercise 9

We could criticize Peter and his team members Martin and Marcel for poor management of activities with slack, for poor communication skills, or for several other project management problems.

However, if we look for the root-cause of the problem it lays on the planning.

Usually, many projects forget to plan for two typical project risks that they may face:

1. **Technical risk**: it is very normal for some machinery not to work as specified by the manual or as expected.
2. **Risk of available resources**: it is ideal to plan thinking that nobody will get sick, no person will have personal problems, no one will leave to work for another company, etc.

14.1 RESOURCES AND TECHNICAL RISKS

During the planning phase of any project, it is necessary to plan for time and resources. The figure below shows a very simple agricultural project through a Gantt chart. It includes the duration and responsible party for each activity.

Task name	Dur	Resource	January	February	...
Agricultural	**60d**				
Land	**30d**				
Buy	10d	John	▇		
Prepare	20d	Charlie	▇▇		
Crops	**30d**				
Plant olives	20d	Mary		▇▇	10d
Plant potatoes	30d	Luis		▇▇▇	
Plant plumbs	10d	Frank		▇	20d

The project's critical activities are shown in red and those with slack are shown in blue. There are only two activities with slack in this project: to plant olive trees, which Maria is a responsible for and planting potatoes by Frank. These activities have a slack of 10 and 20 days, respectively. These slacks indicate the maximum number of days that these activities could be delayed without delaying the project completion day.

This type of planning is the traditional approach for the CPM (Critical Path Method).

Now, if the project manager only performs this analysis to plan his project, he may be in serious trouble.

The critical path method should be complemented with a risk analysis of the critical resources for the project.

It may happen that the activity of planting olive trees, which has a slack of 10 days, is actually an activity with a higher risk or more critical than expected.

What might happen if Maria, an international expert without any replacement, is getting labor offers much better than his actual job?

You got it! Maria could leave and if an urgent replacement for her is not found, which is most likely, the entire project could be delayed because of this activity.

Let's consider now the other activity with a slack of 20 days: planting potatoes.

What might happen if Frank, who has great agricultural experience, is not familiar with the new technology of this crops and this will be his first experience?

You got it again! Frank will need to go through the learning curve. For this reason, an activity that generally an expert completes in 10 days, could take a couple of months longer until the employee learns to use the machines. As a consequence, the whole project would be delayed!

As we can see, activities that have no apparent problems through the critical path, such as those of Maria and Frank, may be the critical activities to consider when planning the project. For this project, Maria represented a risk of resource availability, while Frank's case was a technical risk.

There are two real and tangible reasons for the vast majority of project delays:

- **Lack of adequate resources** to staff critical tasks.
- Failure to recognize and plan for **technical risks**.

Such risks should be considered in the planning of the project, this refers to "shall not forget the critical resources."

Recommendations for managing critical resources:

1. Do not waste time with a detailed plan of the work to be done over the next twelve months. Plan the next three months in detail, do the rest at an aggregate level.
2. Formulate the calendar to execute high-risk tasks as soon as possible, even if these tasks have slack. This way, if delays affect any of these activities, there is still time available to solve whatever the problem is.

Remember that time that is been lost, won't come back!

14.2 CRITICAL RESOURCES

In planning a project it is necessary to pay special attention to those activities that involve critical resources. Both activities in the previous farm example, planting olive trees and potatoes, had slack and were associated to critical resources.

Task name	Dur	Resource	January		February		...
Agricultural	**60d**						
Land	**30d**						
Buy	10d	John	▓▓				
Prepare	20d	Charlie		▓▓▓			
Crops	**30d**						
Plant olives	20d	Mary			▓▓▓		10d
Plant potatoes	30d	Luis		Critical resources	▓▓▓▓		
Plant plumbs	10d	Frank			▓▓		20d

The plum planting activity is part of the critical path, according to CPM, and has no slack days. But maybe is an activity that does not require much attention in relation to the other plantations. This may be the case when such activity has been performed repeatedly within an average of 30 days, with time deviations that never exceeded 2 days. Also, unqualified personnel execute this activity, which could be easily replaced if needed in order to continue with the task.

Those activities that involve risk of human resources availability or technical risk should be managed with extreme caution. Therefore, it is necessary to conduct periodical control on progress status for each activity, to plan activities with a time reserve for contingencies in case of any delay. This contingency reserve is a *buffer* to alleviate the negative impact of the risk factor into the project.

📖 Exercise 10 – Status Control and Risks

It is certain that on this example, Peter Littleluck should have seen in advance what was coming.

His team had started working several months before and since the beginning the progress reports were quite optimistic.

It was supposed to be a project of 4 months, but after 1 month of work the team progress report revealed that only 25% of their tasks had been completed. At 2 months the report said 50%.

At this rate, progress reports seemed so perfect, but in reality there was little real progress in the work. It gives the impression that the last 10% of the project would take 4 additional months. This would delay the project twice as long as planned in relation to the scheduled date. The company had experienced this same situation before for several projects.

What was happening?

Littleluck had given total empowerment to his team, so that they would define the best methods to measure and report the progress status for their projects.

How could you improve this way of controlling and prevent delay risks on a similar project?

✋ 5 minutes. Do not read the answer before thinking of yours.

📖 Answer - Exercise 10

We cannot conduct project monitoring and controlling with only empowerment and trust. Some tips for monitoring and controlling are:

- Define partial deliverables that allow to verify real progress
- Conduct on site audits to see real progress. It is not enough that the technical team sends progress percentages via email. If you cannot travel to the work site, use technology: video cameras, pictures, etc.
- If you are monitoring services where progress is hard to asses, then it is better to use the 20/80 rule: to report 20% of progress if the activity started and the other 80% only if the activity has been finished. It could also be a 0/100 or 50/50 rule, depending on your project.

14.3 MONTE CARLO

Did it ever happen to you that the time planning of your projects is based on inaccurate time estimates from each team member?

Or that it is almost impossible to manage a project with risks of all kinds?

Using the Monte Carlo simulation, we can add time for contingency reserves and assess the risks involved in the activities and critical resources of a project.

The Monte Carlo simulation has its origins in late 1940 with the work done by Stan Ulam and John Von Neumann while investigating the random motion of neutrons. Currently, the Monte Carlo simulation is applied to models used in areas such as IT, finance, economics, and social sciences among others.

The name Monte Carlo comes from the famous city of Monaco, where casinos abound and where gambling, probability and random behavior make an entire lifestyle.

To apply the Monte Carlo simulation into project management, we can use software that analyze different possible scenarios and assess how likely each occurrence is.

By using simulation software, questions such as the following can be answered:

What is the most probable finish date?

What is the probability to finish the project on X date?

What is the most risky path for this project?

For an answer to these questions see Monte Carlo Simulation in Appendix A.

LESSONS LEARNED

While planning for future projects to be managed, it is not enough to work with the critical path method (CPM). This traditional approach should also take into consideration frequent problems faced by projects, such as:

- Risks associated with resources availability.
- Risks associated with the use of new technologies.

It is usually more important to consider what are the critical resources associated with the activities, than to know if an activity is or not part of the critical path.

One tool to incorporate risks of critical resources when planning for contingencies is the Monte Carlo simulation.

15 COMMANDMENT #10

YOU SHALL SANCTIFY PRIORITY PROJECTS

CHAPTER 15

Read the good books first, you might not have a chance to read them all.

HENRY DAVID THOREAU (1817-1862)

American Writer, Poet and Philosopher

We finally reached the last commandment, which mainly refers to focus on those projects that add greater value to the company and to avoid simultaneous work on several tasks without any planning.

15.1 MULTITASKS VERSUS DEDICATED TEAMS

I remember when I worked for Towers Perrin in England, an international leader in actuary consulting, with system and work processes that emulated an ideal company. Each team member was assigned only those activities or projects with high added value that we could develop according to our skills. We had a clear plan for all tasks with specific daily priorities and we were protected against any disturbances.

As a result, work plans were efficiently executed and there was also some spare time to take care of unexpected situations or just to enjoy a better quality of life.

Unfortunately, this does not happen in all organizations. Many of our businesses **do not define priorities** and leave workers helpless to fend for themselves. Many times, the answer we give them when they are extremely busy is "Do it the best you can."

For this reason, employees working on many simultaneous tasks are in a state of constant turmoil and low morale. They cannot add value to any project from their work areas because the phone is constantly ringing, someone is knocking on the door, they get called for another unnecessary meeting, the big boss changed the whole plan again because he dreamed of a bright idea, etc. In soccer terms, several of our companies are asking employees to kick the corner, head the ball and block it, all at the same time. And is most unfortunate when we blame them for missing the goal because they were blocking! ☺

Companies with structures based on projects assign employees to specific projects. Once the employees finish those projects they are re-assigned to another project. Unfortunately, it is not possible or efficient, that all companies work with structures based on projects.

However, to achieve an agile enterprise it is necessary to avoid simultaneous multitasking and to plan activities based on priorities. In addition, you should plan a reserve of time for contingencies. This does not mean to assign employees to work only one project at a time. It simply means that employees will be assigned to high-value tasks to be completed before moving on to another task or project.

This seems trivial, but it is the essence of team **productivity** and value creation. Then, you will see high motivation and morale rising among your employees.

Multitasks	Dedicated Teams
There are no priorities	Prioritize activities
Chronic delays	Reserve for contingencies
Low morale	Create value with high morale
"Do it the best you can"	List of priority projects

Case Guatemala - Excuses to justify multi-projects

Robert Zacapa, a leader of an expansion project of a spirits industry, gave excuses on why workers should learn to handle multiple projects simultaneously. He also said that workers have to learn to live with that necessary evil. Among Robert's main excuses were:

1. As a project leader, it is not my work to manage my team's agendas.

2. My team must also address customer calls and site visits.

3. I have to share my team with other functional managers in the company.

4. We have ten times more projects than our team can handle.

After some training courses in leadership, motivation and project management, Mr. Zacapa changed his attitude and sought answers to each of those excuses.

Answer 1. *Project managers* are paid to solve problems and complete projects in a timely manner. It is necessary that I help my team with prioritizing agendas if we want to finish our projects efficiently.

Answer 2. I must find uninterrupted time to dedicate to the project. In order to do this, we will assign team members to customer-related tasks only, on a rotating and temporary base.

Answer 3. I will negotiate priorities with other functional managers, since it is not possible to perform several projects simultaneously. After all, every member of my team has only two legs, two arms and a head.

Answer 4. If I want to look good with all my clients, I have no choice but to prioritize projects and learn to negotiate longer terms in advance with some of them. I should know the proverb that says, "Don't bite off more than you can chew".

15.2 PLACE FILTERS BETWEEN DISTURBANCES AND THE TEAM

One of the reasons for multitasking originates in the permanent disturbances experienced by some members of the project team. Because of this situation they have very little time for value-added work on the project. These team members have to answer the phones, visit the clients, and listen carefully to senior management ideas during unplanned meetings among many other disturbances.

If only you could place some sort of **filter** between these disturbances and the team, the added value would come by itself. This filter will help your team by preventing distractions from its work plan. These distractions are caused by the disruptive impact of unanticipated requirements of customers and suppliers among others.

For example, in our service business, customer calls are answered until 3:00 PM. That leaves us with two hours every day to focus only on projects. Obviously, there is always an assigned team member, not all, to answer any so-called emergency.

In addition, meetings between senior management and the team are scheduled in advance, respecting the agenda for the day and the time allotted for the meeting.

Another filter could be placed between the team and the changing requirements from the great big boss, as mentioned in the case below.

Case Argentina - Filter between management and the team

A government officer asked us for an integration plan for a major project that would be presented to an international organization. But with a main restriction, the project should be completed in four months, even though it required the support of government staff.

Our answer was a resounding "NO", because in practice a project like this one requires a period of ten months for completion, in an optimistic scenario. We are not even saying what happens in the pessimistic scenario!

The officer offered to assign all staff we needed specifically to this project. Finally, we agreed to do the project, but on two conditions:

1st – The team from the public sector had to come to work to our private offices.

2nd – If any officer needed to go back to the public offices, he must first talk to the project leader to justify the reason.

The officer agreed to both conditions and gave express orders to everyone in the government to respect these.

Once the team was in our office they started with the execution of the project. But not a single day passed when the phone started ringing with urgent requests for the team members. According to the secretaries who called, the requests were all extremely important, so-called "life or death".

Mr. Filter started its main function by addressing these "life or death" calls and not letting the team members get disturb. Fortunately, along the life of the project about 80% of these calls were solved with no problem or need to disturb the team. Only 20% of the calls were referred to the team members. Some examples of these apparent urgent and very important calls that we were able to addressed are:

- Explaining to government staff that team members were working on a very important project and could not perform other activities until completion. Apparently not everyone had heard or understood the express orders from the official.

- Explaining how to use some simple functions in Excel spreadsheets or Word documents.

- Explaining the meaning of terms such as: compound interest, socioeconomic assessment, discount rate, IRR, Project Charter, and WBS among others.

As can be seen, none of these requirements were of "life or death" urgency and no one died until team members returned to their jobs in the public sector.

Thanks to the filter and the high motivation of the team members, who were able to focus on their activities without too much disruption, the project was completed in record time. The project was delivered after two and a half months. It received the funding requested from the international organization and was also praised for the high quality of the presentation and formulation.

Conclusion: The placement of filters to shield our project teams, increases productivity exponentially, meeting or exceeding deadlines that seem impossible.

LESSONS LEARNED

To work on multiple tasks simultaneously without any plan does not correspond to an agile business. Instead, to plan projects with dedicated teams on a priority basis allows adding value to the company.

To fulfill commandment #10, "sanctify priority projects", we should create a list of priority projects or tasks based on the potential of the company and focus resources on those activities with higher added value.

16 BUILDING A SUCCESSFUL PROJECT

There are no secrets to success. It is the result of preparation, hard work, and learning from failure.
COLIN POWELL (1937-?)
American Military and Politician

In the first part of this book we discussed typical problems that are common to our organizations. Then we covered the lean and agile thinking philosophies. Finally, we developed Ten Commandments based on these philosophies, to mitigate the problems of time batches and transaction costs. Now, we will say goodbye by integrating some of these concepts.

16.1 THE VALUE SHEET

The team members in a project can fill a table similar to the one presented below in order to identify and prioritize activities that add large amounts of unnecessary waste or *muda*.

Improvement Initiative	Score (1-3)
Time wasted in meetings	
Delayed achievement of important results	
Outdated project's website	
Time wasted in avoidable errors	
Time wasted in irrelevant tasks	
Poor communications	
Others	

Team members should identify on this table which activities or processes add unnecessary waste to the project.

Also, they should assign a qualitative score to each of the problems identified while taking into consideration how difficult it would be to remove it. For example, the score could be based on a scale of 1 to 3 with the following classification:

1. Difficult to remove.
2. Fairly easy to remove.
3. Easy to remove.

It is recommended to do this analysis biweekly. It should not take more than ten minutes to fill out the table. This management tool provides necessary information to the project manager to be able to apply corrective actions to reduce *muda*, starting with the activities with the higher scores, therefore **easiest to remove**.

You can also ask team members to identify those obstacles to the value stream caused by senior management intervention. The table below shows an example of this management tool.

Improvement Initiative	Score (1-3)
Delay on approvals/decisions	
Poor response to "signals"	
Too much time on status reports	
Lack of resources availability	
Sudden changes to the project charter	
Disturbing micro-management	
Poor communication/Other waste or *muda*	

In this case, the frequency to complete this form may be monthly and anonymously, in order to avoid unnecessary conflicts between staff and management. The main objective with this tool is for senior management to make a self-check. Management will be able to see which of their activities hinder the flow of the project value to eliminate them, starting with the easiest activities to change (the highest score).

Based on these two forms, a general matrix can be constructed to implement corrective actions. We call this new form a *value sheet*. Each of the actions should have a priority. Do not try to solve all the problems at the same time as it is important for team members to see *agile* changes in the project management. Therefore, it is fundamental to begin solving the easiest action to change.

Improvement Initiative	Score (1-3)
Time wasted in meetings	
Delayed achievement of important results	
Outdated project's website	
Time wasted in avoidable errors	
Time wasted in irrelevant tasks	
Poor communications	
Others	

Priority	Action

Improvement Initiative	Score (1-3)
Delay on approvals/decisions	
Poor response to "signals"	
Too much time on status reports	
Lack of resources availability	
Sudden changes to the project charter	
Disturbing micro-management	
Poor communication/Other waste or *muda*	

16.2 THE COMMANDMENTS PYRAMID

The following figure summarizes the 10 commandments that an agile leader should always have in mind.

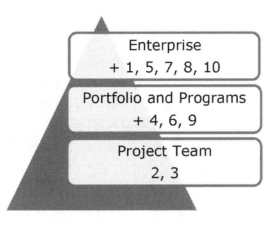

If you want to implement efficient actions within the project team then focus on commandments 2 and 3. If you are managing a portfolios or programs, then pay more attention to the commandments 4, 6 and 9, in addition to the ones listed for the team. Finally, if you're looking for an agile company, then you will have no choice but to pay careful attention to the Ten Commandments!

The 10 commandments

I. Do not add... **waste and *muda*** to the project
II. Honor... deliverables for the **client**
III. Do not loose... time in **meetings**
IV. Do not forget... **risk** analysis
V. Lift... **traditional** stages
VI. Covet... **visual** methods
VII. Do not kill... standard **processes**
VIII. Do not cause... long **waits**
IX. Do not forget... critical **resources**
X. Sanctify... **priority** projects

By Paul Leido

We were asked once "which is the most important commandment of all? And "with which one should I start?". There is a very simple answer that covers all the commandments: **"Love the customer above all things."**

This last commandment is the foundation for achieving successful projects.

16.3 TRADICIONAL MANAGEMENT VERSUS AGILE

In **traditional project management** you can find the following characteristics:

- Proposals are full of waste or *muda*.
- There are unnecessary delays because of batches in the flow of value.
- Coordination and collaboration meetings tale longer than necessary
- In some extreme cases there are eternal meetings.
- Companies praise and support the management strategies of heroes and super-geniuses, owners of the information.
- Time, costs and quality estimates are based on the ODM (oscillating digits method) or the TGE (team's good eye).
- Risks management and planning are not taken into consideration.
- Planning is based only on the critical path, in the best scenario.
- Bureaucratic processes usually have a FIFO (first-in-first-out) system.
- It is normal to work in an environment of simultaneous *multitasks*.
- It requires high wear and tear to achieve the objectives.

On the contrary, in an **agile project management** system the following characteristics are present:

- Proposals are focused on the clients' needs without adding additional waste or *muda*.
- The project's value stream is identified and an agile environment is created so there are no interruptions to it.
- Teams are committed with the project and owners of the information are not well seen by the organization.
- Work is based on processes.
- Planning and risk management are taken into consideration in projects.
- It expands the vision of the critical path to include critical resources associated with each activity.
- It works with a system where reservations are planned, with a system of turns to avoid lines and waiting.
- All activities of the programs and projects are planned and prioritized in order to avoid simultaneous multitasking.
- Good results are achieved with higher quality of life, in relation to traditional management.

The following figure summarizes the differences between the traditional and the agile projects management approaches.

Traditional Management	Agile Management
Batches and transaction costs	Value stream
Eternal meetings	Efficient meetings
Information owner / firemen	Compromised Teams
ODM / TGE	Processes
High risk	Risks management
Critical path	Critical resources
Bureaucracy and waits	Turns y reservations
Multitasking	Tasks prioritization
High **wear and tear**	**Quality of Life**

Case Wear versus Life

Even though some projects can work with somewhat not well-organized processes and with little lean-agile thinking, many entrepreneurs can be praised for their great adaptability to constant changes within their work context. Thanks to this flexibility and entrepreneurial drive, projects are successful, regardless of not having *efficient* processes implemented.

However, this permanent system of improvisation and disorder forces the project team members to achieve excellent results at the expense of unnecessary overexertion.

How many weekends we had to stay to work on the project? How many times we left the office later than normal? How much is worth to get home late and find that the kids are already sleeping?

Several of the projects we are involved with are surrounded by little lean-agile processes. For this reason, it is usual for team members in this environment to work an average of fifty hours minimum per week in order to achieve good results.

Those of us, who have had the opportunity to work on similar projects in a more efficient culture, also achieved excellent results. But with a big difference: a much better quality of life as a result of working in a planned and efficient environment!

For example, when I use to live in England, it was usual to work a maximum of thirty two hours per week. You may ask, how did you got to this figure? We worked eight hours a day for four days a week. Our company granted one day off per week so we can stay at home and study for the actuarial certification. The company policy also forbade employees to work more than eight hours per day. Even though we worked less hours per week it was surprising the level of productivity achieved. The satisfaction of having completed a business day earlier and with high productivity levels was very motivating. Therefore, the rest of the day could be devoted to family, friends and sports without a guilty conscience.

> Why not try to create a more agile environment in your projects?
> We assure you that the *agile* management is much easier than the *traditional* world and the reward of a better quality of life will be worth the attempt.

Anti-Murphy's Law

Everything that you want to happen in your project can really happen. Work with dedication, agility and efficiency so that luck is on your side.

Finally, it is not necessary to implement all the commandments. It would be enough if some of these ideas have served you to detect where in your project is the waste or *muda* that can be easily eliminated.

If you can eliminate only 10% of *muda* from your project, that will result in: the addition of approximately ten minutes of added-value time worked daily; your company could accomplish 10% more of the projects; a 10% faster project; or 10% cheaper. In other words, you could quickly get a 10% return over the same resources and with less effort. So what are you waiting for: **Let's get to work!**

LESSONS LEARNED

The project team should identify those activities that generate *muda*, both caused by the project itself or by management.

Then, priorities should be established in order to eliminate *muda*, starting with those activities that are easiest to change.

It is necessary to apply the 10 agile commandments in order to achieve an agile enterprise. It is worth the try and to enjoy the benefits of a better quality of life!

PART IV

APPENDICES

Appendix A - @RISK

A
P
P
E
N
D
I
X

A

"Man is still the most extraordinary computer of all."
JOHN FITZGERALD KENNEDY (1917-1963)
American Politician

In order to use the Monte Carlo simulation in project management we can use the *@Risk* software developed by *Palisade* enterprise. This software is based in the Monte Carlo simulation to analyze possible different scenarios and to evaluate how probable it is for each scenario to occur.

📖 Exercise 11 – Schedule Risk

Peter Littleluck learned his lesson and decided to change the way he will manage his future projects with similar characteristics. The starting date for a project is **July 1, 2020** (1/7/20).

A.1. CONTINGENCY RESERVE

After acknowledging that some project activities may be at risk of resource availability and/or technological risk, experts meet to estimate 3 dates for each activity of the "Install one generator" project.

Task name	Optimistic duration	Duration	Pessimistic duration	Jan	Feb	Mar	Apr	May	Jun
Project	**130 d.**	**170 d.**	**285 d.**						
Plan	20 d.	30 d.	50 d.	▓					
Install	80 d.	100 d.	160 d.		▓	▓	▓		
Test	30 d.	40 d.	75 d.					▓	

With this information you choose to add a contingency reserve.

What is the estimated end date for the project?

With this information, instead of planning your project with the most probable duration of 170 days, you can add a contingency reserve in case of a schedule delay by using the *@Risk* software.

These are the 10 basic steps to follow in order to add a contingency reserve to the project:

1st Develop your project into a Microsoft Project template.

Project	170 d	01/01/20	25/08/20
PLAN	30 d	01/01/20	11/02/20
INSTALL	100 d	12/02/20	30/06/20 1
TEST	40 d	01/07/20	25/08/20 2

Note: add the project summary task from Format and click "Show project summary task".

2nd Run the software *@Risk*.  The tools bar is shown as an Add-Ins for Excel.

3rd Don´t close Project. From Excel, click in "Project / Project Link / Read Active Project". Now your project will be at the Excel spreadsheet in order to undertake the Monte Carlo simulation.

4th Click over the cell that will be assigned a probability distribution; i.e. over the duration estimate of the 30 days for the *Plan* activity. Click on the *Define Distributions* icon and select the probability distribution Pert (this is one of the best distributions when we have 3 duration's estimates).

5ᵗʰ Fill the Pert fields with the estimated durations: min. 20 days (optimistic), most likely 30 days and max. 50 days (pessimistic). On this particular case, the graphic shows that there is a 90% probability that this activity will be within 23.28 and 41.40 days. Click on *Apply*.

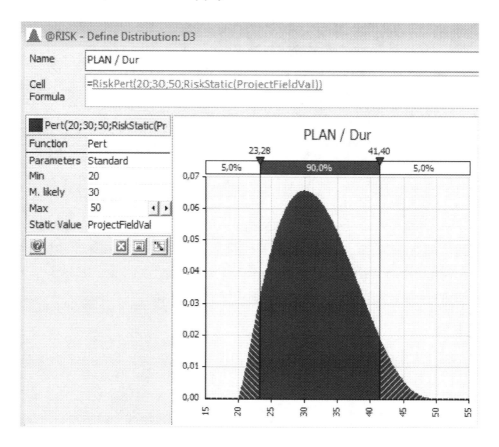

6ᵗʰ Repeat steps 4 and 5 for all the other activities.

- Install: optimistic 80 days, most probable 100 days, pessimistic 160 days.
- Test: optimistic 30 days, most probable 40 days, pessimistic 75 days.

7ᵗʰ Click over the cell for which the contingency reserve will be estimated, for this example it will be the 170 days duration estimate. Click on *Add Outputs* / OK.

	A	B	C	D	E	F	G	H	L	M	N
1	ID		Task	Dur	Start						
2	0		Project	170 d	1/1/2020						
3	1		PLAN	30 d	1/1/2020						
4	2		INSTALL	100 d	12/2/2020	30/6/2020	1				
5	3		TEST	40 d	1/7/2020	25/8/2020	2				

Ribbon fields:
- Iterations: 100
- Simulations: 1

@RISK - Add/Edit Output: Cell D2

Name: Project / Dur

Remove   OK   Cancel

D2 — fx 170

8th Fill the field *Iterations* with the number of simulations that will be run for this model. For example, 1000 iterations or more will give excellent statistical information.

9th Click on *Start Simulation*. The software will choose random durations for each activity within the selected probability distribution limits, and it will calculate the duration for the project. This process will be repeated 1000 times.

Start Simulation

10th Once the 1000 iterations are done, the statistics are obtained for the duration of the project. For this particular case, the project may take 182.5 days (see *Mean* on right-hand-side box). This is the average value obtained after the simulation of 1000 iterations for the possible durations of each activity.

Therefore, instead of planning for this project with a duration estimate of 170 days, as it appears on the initial plan, it should be planned for 182.5 days and have a contingency reserve of 13 additional days (183-170). But even this reserve could be low, because the probability for this project to be finished on 182.5 days or less is only 50%. If the team wants greater certainty of not having any delay, then the contingency reserve should be larger. For example, the statistics obtained also show that 95% of the simulations presented a 212.2 days or less (see 212.2 on the right–upper part of the graph).

If you are following this exercise on your own PC and see different values for the 1000 iterations, please remember that there could be a reasonable difference of +/- 1 day because your 1000 iterations are different.

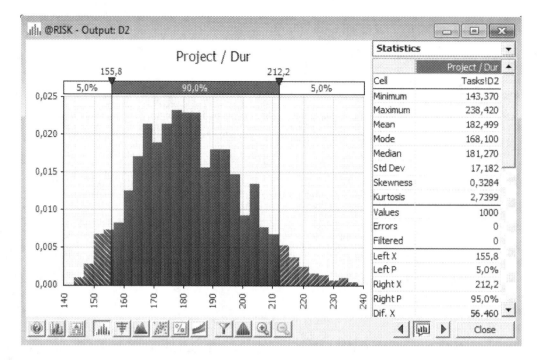

If the project manager works with an estimate of 212 days, 42 additional days to the original plan, then the project will have a 95% probability of finishing on schedule.

If there is an interest of estimating the reserve with a probability different than 50% or 95%, previously explained, then move the vertical bar on the right of the graph to find the desired probability. It is important to note that there is a 5% already from the origin to the vertical bar on the left of the graph.

The graph below shows an example for a contingency reserve that covers 80% of the scenarios. In other words, this reserve would expose 20% of the risk. The graph shows that there is an 80% probability to complete this project in 197 days or less.

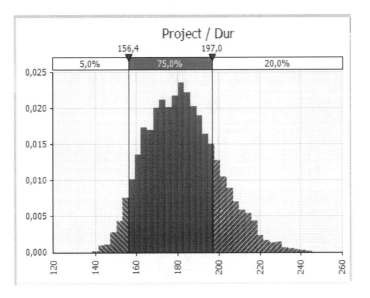

What would have happened if we left the original planning of 170 days?

There is only a 25.5% probability for this project to be completed in 170 days or less.

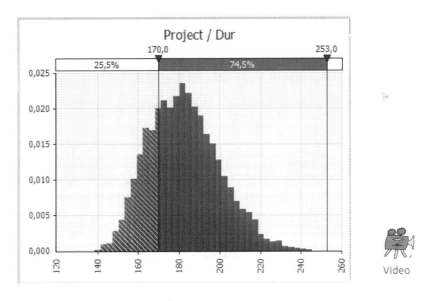

Video

Bingo! You are now able to estimate contingency reserves for your projects or you are in a better position to ask your company technicians to use these tools to better plan the projects' schedules.

A.2. PARALLEL PATHS

On this occasion, our renowned Peter Littleluck should plan the same project discussed in the previous section, but with a change: there are three identical generators instead of one. The figure below outlines the project.

Task name	Optimistic duration	Duration	Pessimistic duration	Jan	Feb	Mar	Apr	May	Jun
Project x 3	**130 d.**	**170 d.**	**285 d.**						
Generator 1	**130 d.**	**170 d.**	**285 d.**						
Plan 1	20 d.	30 d.	50 d.	▓					
Install 1	80 d.	100 d.	160 d.		▓	▓	▓		
Test 1	30 d.	40 d.	75 d.					▓	
Generator 2	**130 d.**	**170 d.**	**285 d.**						
Plan 2	20 d.	30 d.	50 d.	▓					
Install 2	80 d.	100 d.	160 d.		▓	▓	▓		
Test 2	30 d.	40 d.	75 d.					▓	
Generator 3	**130 d.**	**170 d.**	**285 d.**						
Plan 3	20 d.	30 d.	50 d.	▓					
Install 3	80 d.	100 d.	160 d.		▓	▓	▓		
Test 3	30 d.	40 d.	75 d.					▓	

As you can see, this three generators project should also be finalized in 170 days, same as the project for one generator.

Does this planning have common sense?

How is it possible that a project with one generator and three activities would take the same amount of time than a project with three generators and nine activities?

I know! Those who are too fast to answer say that it is fine for the duration of the project to stay the same because there are three parallel paths. However, this response lacks statistical logic. It is not possible for a project with few activities to last the same as one with three times the activities. The probability of something going wrong in a project increases when the number of activities on the project increases.

Therefore, as the number of activities in a project increases, so does the probability of a delay.

Again, the traditional approach to the critical path does not solve the problem. We should use the Monte Carlo simulation in order to be more accurate on the planning process for this project and fix this problem.

What is the most probable duration for this project?

What would be the maximum number of days for this project with a 95% probability?

The statistics shown in the figure below are obtain when repeating all Monte Carlo simulation steps explained on the previous section.

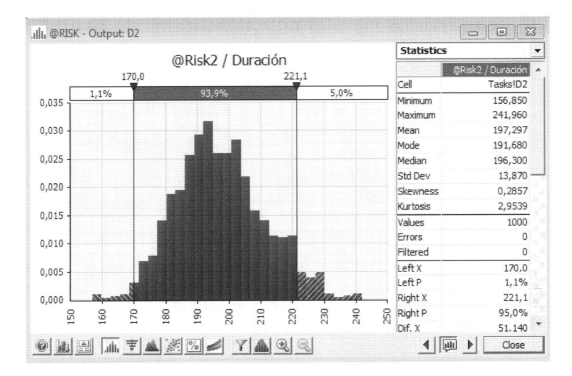

The most probable duration for this project is 197 days. Meanwhile there is a 95% probability that the project would take 221 days or less for completion. Therefore, adding a contingency reserve of 51 days (221-170) would allow for only a 5% chance of a project delay.

You can see that the estimated dates for the project are not just larger than the traditional approach of the critical path (170 days), but also, these estimates are larger than the estimates for the project with one generator (most probable duration was 183 days and 212 days covered 95% of the scenarios).

Finally, the probability of completing the project in 170 days or less, as stated in the original plan is only 1% and **that is impossible.**

Here is a great lesson, when using traditional techniques that do not take into consideration critical resources, risks and contingency reserves into their schedules, we are signing the death certificate of a project that certainly will not be successful and has not even begun.

A.3. PARALLEL PATHS RISKS

For their new *three generators* project, Peter and his work team developed a schedule with a higher level of detail and the following dates:

Task name	Optimistic duration	Duration	Pessimistic duration	Jan	Feb	Mar	Apr	May	Jun
Project x 3		**173 d.**							
Generator 1	**136 d.**	**169 d.**	**269 d.**						
Plan 1	19 d.	29 d.	49 d.						
Install 1	85 d.	100 d.	150 d.						
Test 1	32 d.	40 d.	70 d.						
Generator 2	**153 d.**	**173 d.**	**223 d.**						
Plan 2	28 d.	33 d.	43 d.						
Install 2	90 d.	100 d.	125 d.						
Test 2	35 d.	40 d.	55 d.						
Generator 3	**127 d.**	**167 d.**	**282 d.**						
Plan 3	17 d.	27 d.	47 d.						
Install 3	80 d.	100 d.	160 d.						
Test 3	30 d.	40 d.	75 d.						

According to the Critical Path Method, the second generator activities determine the critical path, while the activities related to the first and third generator have slack.

> Does this mean that we only have to be mindful of the critical path?

Not necessarily. The project manager and his team can perform a detailed analysis for all the activities and find that those activities with slack have technical and resources availability risks.

> Which of the three paths has higher risk?

@Risk can be used to perform 1000 simulations for this project and then evaluate which of the three generators hit the critical path the most.

These are the steps to accomplish this:

1st Repeat steps discussed previously and include the new durations (optimistic, most probable and pessimistic) for each activity of the project.

2nd Click on the tab *Project / Project Settings and click Calculate Critical Indices.*

Project Settings

Simulation | General |

During Simulation

☑ Calculate Critical Indices

☑ Calculate Statistics for Probabilistic Gantt Chart

☐ Collect Timescaled Data

3rd Click on *Start Simulation*.

4th Once all 1000 iterations are finished, click on *Project / Charts and Reports / Probabilistic Gantt* / OK.

5th Search in the column Critical Index the results. This example's results show that after 1000 iterations, the first generator activities were 36.3% of the iterations on the critical path. The second generator activities were part of the critical path around 26.1% and the activities of the third generator were critical the remaining 37.6% of the time. Therefore, it can be concluded that the activities for the first and third generators are riskier than the second generator's activities.

	A	B	K	L	M	N	O	P	Q	R	S	T	U	V
1	ID	Task	Critical Index%	Jan	Feb	Mar	Apr	May	Jun	Jul	Aug	Sep	Oct	Nov
2	0	Program	n/a											
3	1	Project 1	n/a											
4	2	PLAN 1	36,30%											
5	3	INSTALL 1	36,30%											
6	4	TEST 1	36,30%											
7	5	Project 2	n/a											
8	6	PLAN 2	26,10%											
9	7	INSTALL 2	26,10%											
10	8	TEST 2	26,10%											
11	9	Project 3	n/a											
12	10	PLAN 3	37,60%											
13	11	INSTALL 3	37,60%											
14	12	TEST 3	37,60%											

Again, this analysis demonstrates that the traditional Critical Path Method is necessary, but not enough, to manage projects efficiently.

After running the software @Risk, the activities in Project could not be linked properly. For example:

1	A	5 d
2	B	10 d
3	C	15 d

To solve this bug without closing Microsoft Project, we should follow these steps: File / Options / Schedule / Calculation / Calculate project after each edit: **On**.

Now, the activities correlation will be correct.

Congratulations, you have just finished reading the technical part of this book.

APPENDIX B – SCRUM

*Offense wins games, but defense and a good scrum
win championships*
PABLO LANGYEDOT (1971 - ?)
Rugby player

<u>Author</u>: Cecilia Boggi, PMP
Degree in Systems
President of ActivePMO

When we mention **SCRUM** it seems like an acronym for "Software Cycle Review Unified Methodology" or "Software Creation Require Users Method". [8] But it really has nothing to do with these names because the term *Scrum* comes from **rugby**. It is the name of the circular interlaced formation formed by the members of both teams while pushing to win the ball.

---

[8] GABAY, Alejandro. (2011) "Metodologías Agiles de Dirección de Proyectos", ORT, Buenos Aires.

The *scrum* is a way of restarting play in rugby football after an accidental infringement. In *scrum* the rugby ball is held between the two rival teams and no one knows who will have the ball or to which direction the attack will take. The team will have to adapt quickly to an offensive or defensive play depending on who has managed to get the ball.

The methodology known as *Scrum* was not born in the software industry as many believe. It has its origin in an article written in 1986 by Takeuchi and Nonata. This article described an approach used in manufacturing processes that accelerated the development of new products. This approach was also tested in the automotive industry and in the manufacture of cameras, computers and printers. In their article, Takeuchi and Nonaka compared the proposed manufacturing process, which is performed by a multifunctional team with overlapping phases among them, with the game of rugby.

In the decade of the 90s, Ken Schwaber and Jeff Sutherland, individually, implemented these concepts in the development of software. They also presented several articles about this software in the 1995 OOPSLA[9] that was held in Austin. Later, they worked together to consolidate the concepts they developed in their articles and their experiences, under the name of *Scrum*.

In 2001, Schwaber and Sutherland were among those who signed the Agile Manifesto in Utah.

In 2002, Ken Schwaber was already the author of several books on *Scrum*. He partnered with Mike Cohn and founded the **Scrum Alliance**, which initially was part of the **Agile Alliance**.

Up until now, a large number of renowned companies have adopted *Scrum* for their software development processes. We can mention, among many others: IBM, Apple, Microsoft, Yahoo, Electronic Arts, Google, Siemens, Nokia, John Deere, BBC, Time Warner, etc.

---

[9] OOPSLA: "Object-Oriented Programming, Systems, Languages & Applications" is an annual research and development conference on object-oriented programming that takes place in the United States.

B.1 SCRUM FUNDAMENTALS

Scrum is an agile and structured framework that allows software development teams to work with their customers in order to develop innovative and complex products in an environment of trust and few simple rules. This framework proposes a reduction of traditional methodologies that flourished in the 90's and could be considered "too heavy".

The **concepts** underlying *Scrum* are:

- In experimental projects, predictive methods are less effective than iterative or incremental approaches that provide client with early results, which allows her to make corrections.

- Professional and skilled teams thrive and produce better results if they work in self-managed teams where everyone takes responsibility for their work and commits to quality by following their own processes.

- Projects that have constant collaboration with the client and sponsor are more likely to succeed than those projects in which stakeholders are only involved at the beginning of the project and at the end to approve or reject the final product or service. By having a constant collaboration, changes to requirements can be quickly detected and incorporated to the next iterations of the project. This will assure a final product that is aligned to the needs of the customer and business.

Scrum is based on an incremental-iterative lifecycle. It aims to optimize predictability and control risk. In *Scrum* each iteration is called "**sprint**" and has a fixed duration of 2 to 4 weeks. During this period, the selected work is done and at the end of each sprint a software product is obtained. This product provides some expected functionality to the customer.

To define the expected functionalities to be developed in the project, the client or user's requirements are defined. These requirements are called "**user stories**" and specify, in a narrative format, how the client or user will work with the software. Prioritization is done by evaluating the user stories according to the value they provide to the customer's business and the risk inherent in each one. The stories with greater value and risks are developed in the first sprints.

The set of all the functionalities that need to be developed, i.e. the set of all user stories, is called the "**Product Backlog**". The set of all the stories to be developed on each sprint is called "**Sprint Backlog**".

During the sprint, each team member takes a user story and develops it. When finished, he continues with another user story and so on until the end of the sprint.

Scrum Framework

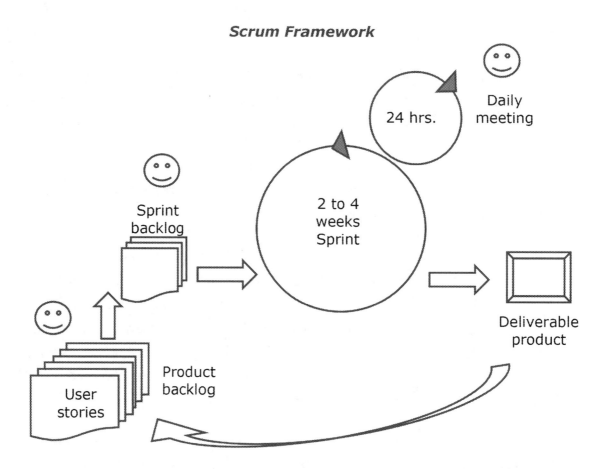

When the sprint comes to term, there will be a software product to validate with the user or client and get feedback. The remarkable thing about this way of working is that the user's feedback comes at a very early stage in the development process, since the sprint lasts at least 4 weeks. This fact offers a great strategy for managing stakeholder's expectations.

B.2 SCRUM COMPONENTS

Scrum comprises three roles, four ceremonies and three artifacts.

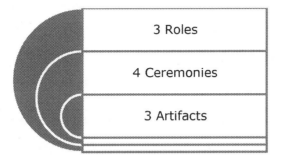

The Three Roles of Scrum

Scrum projects define three principal roles: the Product Owner, the Scrum Master and the Scrum Team.

| Product Owner | Scrum Master | Scrum Team |

The **Product Owner** is the person who represents the interests of the user or customer and ensures that the product developed meets its needs. The Product Owner defines and prioritizes the functionality and features of the product. It is responsible for determining the product's value to the business and prioritizes the features based on the value it provides to the business. The owner is also responsible for accepting or rejecting work results.

The **Scrum Master** is a boundary manager who is responsible for the development process. It provides support to the development team, isolates it from external interference and solves problems that may arise along the way. This will ensure that the team works properly and is highly productive. Overall, it is a technical specialist who is responsible for the architecture and quality of the project development.

The **Scrum Team** consists of 5 to 9 persons who usually work full time on the project. This team integrates interdisciplinary professionals such as programmers, user interface designers, database administrators, and staff responsible for testing, among others. These team members are responsible for executing the development of the product with the required quality. Scrum teams are self-managed and have the authority to make decisions deemed appropriate. For this reason, it is required that team members are highly trained and skilled.

These are the three core roles in any Scrum environment and are often referred to as "**pigs**". Others involved in the development project are called "**chickens**". These labels come from a story whose protagonists are a pig and a chicken [10]

Story – The chicken and the pig

One day a pig and a chicken are walking down the road. The chicken greets the pig and makes a proposal: *"Hey pig, I was thinking we should open a restaurant!"*

Pig looks at the chicken and replies: *"Sounds like a good idea. And what would we call it?"*

The Chicken thinks for a while and responds: *"How about 'ham & eggs'?"*

The Pig thinks for a moment and says: *"No thanks. I'd be committed, but you'd only be involved!"*

HAM & EGGS

---

[10] Adapted from the book "Agile Management", from C.P. Puri, Global India Publications, 2009.

The "pigs" roles are those who are truly committed with the development of the project and the *Scrum* process. These are the three roles that were defined earlier: Product Owner, Scrum Master and Scrum Team.

The "chicken" roles are those who are not directly involved in the development process but are also important for the project. These are the users, business experts and other stakeholders who are involved and provide feedback to the product after each sprint.

The Four Ceremonies of Scrum

Scrum calls ceremonies to **meetings** taking place in the project life cycle. There are four ceremonies: the Sprint planning meeting, the daily Scrum meeting, the Sprint review meeting, and the Sprint retrospective.

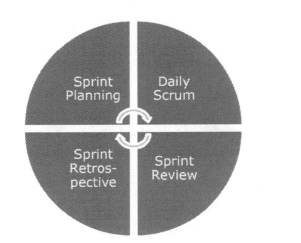

Sprint Planning

This meeting is held prior to the start of the Sprint. The main objective is to define the work to be done and the objectives to be pursued in the Sprint. The user stories to be included in the Sprint are selected from the Product Backlog. This process is based on prioritization depending on the value the stories provide to the business and the risks inherent in them.

Scrum Daily Meeting

This is the follow-up meeting on the progress of the Sprint. It is done daily, always at the same time, for no more than fifteen minutes and everyone stays standing.

The purpose of this meeting is to review the progress of each task, and the work planned for the day. This meeting is open to anyone, but only the Scrum Team, the Scrum Master and the Product Owner have permission to speak.

Each member responds in a concise way to three questions:

- What work has been done since last meeting?
- What work will be done until next meeting?
- What problems or challenges are foreseen in order to complete the work?

Issues and problems are not resolved during the daily Scrum meeting. These issues get scheduled to be addressed by those who are directly affected in a later meeting. This short daily meeting avoids other unnecessary meetings.

Sprint Review

During the Sprint Review meeting the team presents the work done during the Sprint. The team prepares a demonstration of the features developed without using slideshows. Usually, all the team members participate and all stakeholders are invited.

Sprint Retrospective

After the end of each Sprint the team meets to debrief what worked well and what aspects should be improved. This ceremony lasts 15 to 30 minutes and is called the Sprint Retrospective.

The team discusses and identifies:

- What they need to start doing
- What they need to stop doing
- What they need to continue doing

The Three Scrum Artifacts

Scrum uses three artifacts or basic elements: the Product Backlog, the Sprint Backlog and the Sprint Burndown Chart.

Product Backlog

The Product Backlog is the inventory of features that the Product Owner wants as the result of the project. It is prioritized according to the value that each functionality provides to the business. It contains all project requirements defined by the Product Owner, as required by the Client or User, at the beginning of the project, and in the form of User Stories.

User Stories contain a narrative description of how the user or client will work with the software. These stories will also be used to plan, estimate and prioritize work. They also contain test and acceptance criteria that will determine if the development of each User Story has been completed. [11]

While planning, the Scrum Team will estimate the development effort for each User Story. It may be either in hours or units of measure called "Story Points", which indicate their relative size.

The Product Backlog is a living document. This means that features can be added and removed as a result of emerging changes in business needs and priorities. These features are reviewed at the beginning of each Sprint. The Product Backlog is available to all persons involved in the project. Everyone can contribute and make suggestions but the Product Owner is responsible for the Product Backlog.

---

[11] Adapted from the book "User Stories Applied for Agile Software Development", by Mike Cohn, Addison –Wesley, 2004.

Sprint Backlog

The Sprint Backlog contains the features that will be developed in the current Sprint.

Based on the priorities designated by the Product Owner, the team selects the features that may be developed during the Sprint period. This selection is based on the estimates of those functionalities and how fast the team works on its development. These selected functionalities will compose the Sprint Backlog.

During the development of each Sprint the team members choose from the Sprint Backlog the tasks that they will work on. Once they finish working with that task, they choose another task and so on, until the Sprint is completed.

The remaining work of the Sprint is estimated every day. This remaining work is represented in a diagram called Sprint Burndown Chart.

During the Sprint development, the Sprint Backlog does not allow for changes or additions, unless defined by the Scrum Team. Any changes will impact the Product Backlog and will be incorporated into future Sprints, according to their prioritization.

Sprint Burndown Chart

The Sprint Burndown Chart is a diagram used by the Scrum Team to track work progress for each Sprint. It is a graph that shows a day-by-day estimated value of the remaining work of the Sprint Backlog.

At the beginning of the Sprint, the value of the graph represents the number of hours or Story Points estimated for all the user stories within the Sprint.

As user stories are developed, hours or "burned" story points are subtracted, until the end of the Sprint.

The goal of each Sprint is to get to the deadline, which is always fixed, with the Burndown Chart at zero. Otherwise, there will be pending user stories to re-prioritize for the planning of the next Sprint.

B.3 HOW TO ADOPT SCRUM

It seems that some organizations choose to venture into agile methodologies in general, and *Scrum* in particular, without being prepared for it. Sometimes, project teams adopt *Scrum* out of curiosity and other times because they believe that these new methodologies will solve the problems of their project.

In general, these organizations incorporate some of the *Scrum* practices in their projects, such as: Product and Sprint Backlogs, daily meetings, and short intervals of development cycles similar to the Sprints. In such cases, the improvements are relatively small if they occur at all. Also, these improvements will not compensate for the problems created by the new way of working on an organizational culture that is not ready to change.

On the other hand, there are some other organizations that understand that change needs an **appropriate culture** within the organization. It does not involve a superficial modification of certain practices that only affect programmers or the technical team.

Success in adopting a *Scrum* management model does not depend on the professional level and responsibility of the Scrum Master. It neither depends on having a highly skilled and motivated team, or the best Product Owners. It requires that the culture of the organization and its projects are consistent with the model.

Management will need to provide resources for the implementation and operation of agile practices and adequate training of both, the team and stakeholders. It is crucial that customers or end users understand their important role and participation in the project.

The implementation and operation of *Scrum* should be continually **monitored**. This will allow identifying issues affecting the team and impeding it to achieve the goal for the Sprint. It also allows identifying organizational practices or decisions that hinder the process in this *Scrum* methodology.

There are some problems that will emerge during the implementation of *Scrum*. These are related to management or stakeholders needing to have a complete and detailed plan at the beginning of the project, an almost fixed scope estimate, and final schedule and project costs. In other words, they need or want a predictive model. If this is the case, it will be necessary to "convince" management about the benefits of the model before you can start any work.

It is common to find some skills deficiency and lack of staff knowledge during the first experiences with *Scrum*. In the *Scrum* model the **team is self-managed**. This means that team members must be highly motivated, ready to auto-assign work and willing to commit to its development. Lack of motivation, commitment, communication and technical skills in the team will result in obstacles to carrying out a successful project.

During the adoption of *Scrum*, it is necessary to consider that the client or product end user have to have full understanding of how the project scope will be managed. What does this mean? We have said that the Product Backlog definition and documentation is done at the initial planning of the project. These processes include the definition of all requirements and its documentation in the form of user stories. Clients may expect that all defined stories will be developed during the period established for the project. However, this may not be true. As the project progresses and changes are welcome, the user stories that provide greater value to the business will be included in the following Sprints. It may happen that some of the stories defined at the beginning are not included in the final product or at least in the current product release. If the client is not aware of this detail then it will usually expect all the features defined in the Product Backlog to be developed, as well as all the changes that emerged during the course of the project. This situation will generate conflict and client's dissatisfaction.

One way to demonstrate the value of the *Scrum* model is to start with the implementation of its practices into a pilot project. It is recommended that the selected project is critical to the business in order to demonstrate the benefits of delivering features early. It is important to consider training all participants, customers and key users on the model. They are the ones who will support and bear witness to the benefits.

The adoption of Scrum is an effort of the company

in all its dimensions.

APPENDIX C – KANBAN

__Never__ give up on a dream.
Just try to see the signs that lead you to it.
PAULO COELHO (1947-?)
Brazilian Writer

Author: **Esteban Zuttion, MBA, CSDP (IEEE)**
Systems Engineer
Technology Manager at Neuralsoft

C.1 THE BEGINNINGS OF KANBAN

Kanban means **sign or signboard** in Japanese. It is the name given to the mechanism implemented through a card that flows from the moment an order is received until the job is finished. The Kanban card contains all the information needed so that each intermediate point in the process knows which task needs to process.

Kanban is used as an essential part of Lean, which emerged in the 1940s as a production paradigm introduced by Toyota in Japan. It was based on an opposition to the mass production schemes of the large American manufacturers. The challenge was to achieve low production costs, because by that time, people in Japan did not have many resources and the country had a much smaller market when compared with American companies. These American companies were based on mass production lines where they made cars for a large volume market and as a result this allowed to considerably lower costs. The challenge for Toyota was to lower the production costs, but with much lower volumes.

As a result of this need, the Toyota Production System was born and conceived by Taiichi Ohno.

What were the results?

Through the introduction of innovative ways of production, the Japanese industry achieved a 50% reduction in engineering effort and managed to reduce production time by one-third when compared to traditional approaches. These results demonstrated that changes in the final stages of production were better than the changes made during the design stage.

To reduce production costs, American companies developed their production processes in series and allowed little participation from the suppliers. As a result, these companies had long production processes in order to integrate users' needs into the early stages of the process and incorporate changes at the beginning of it. On the other hand, Japanese companies honored fast development, shortening the production cycle, and leaving the design decisions for the final stages of development.

"Do not make a decision on what will be developed until you have an order. Then, design the product as quickly as possible"

The model followed by Japanese companies was Lean Development and was adopted by several companies around the world in the late 90's.

C.2 THE BEGINNINGS OF LEAN DEVELOPMENT

These are the principles used by Lean Development:

- **Waste elimination**: anything that does not add value to the customer is considered a waste. For example: all wait or delay, interim storing, transport, extra step, etc.
- **Amplify learning**: generate short cycles that provide learning opportunities for decision making and the improvement on the cycle.
- **Make design decisions as late as possible**: simultaneous development over sequential development.
- **Perform deliveries as quickly as possible**: reducing work in progress, delivering fast, and reducing risk. Implementation of a "Pull" system.
- **"Empower" the team**: to achieve a motivated team with leadership over controlled management.
- **Develop a robust and comprehensive product**: balancing between functionality, usability, reliability and economy in order to achieve satisfied users.
- **See the whole**: systemic view of the development process with dynamic systems and the use of measurements.

The mechanism called Kanban originates within what Lean proposes as "Pull System" and under the use of the concepts of "Just in Time". It serves as a basis for coordinating the work of the company employees. It also helps with the whole mechanism of relating with the suppliers of the parts needed for making the products ordered.

C.3 KANBAN IN SOFTWARE DEVELOPMENT

The software development process can be seen under the same standards used to analyze a production process like the ones implemented by Japanese automakers during recent decades.

The use of "Kanban" in software development is implemented through a board displaying the "work orders" to be processed.

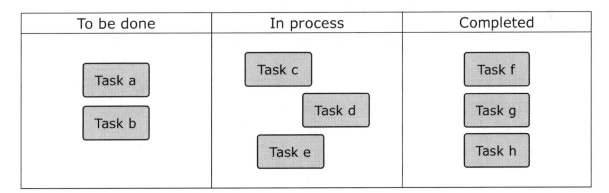

To be done	In process	Completed
Task a Task b	Task c Task d Task e	Task f Task g Task h

This board implements the requests' list "to be done" (backlog) of what that needs to be processed. These features are similar to those described for Scrum, where requests are implemented on cards and managed through a board. From this board, team members "remove" (pull) those requests that will be processed and worked until completion.

Development Process

The development process can be seen as a system of queues (work-lists) that occur at different times during the process. These queues, or lists, store work orders, or requests, between the different stages of the development cycle. When these work queues start to grow, slowing down tasks, the development cycle times begin to stretch and completion of the request is delayed. The problems causing the delay may include an overload of work at one stage of the cycle. For example, it could happen that during the analysis, it is needed to finish some "parts" of the product in order to proceed with the process. This may imply, for example, completing the list of testing cases for a request in order to start with the testing.

As seen before, one of the Lean principles is to reduce the work cycle. In this context, the challenge translates into how to minimize those "queues" of intermediate orders so that the operation flows dynamically without slowing down the development cycle. To find out to what extent this goal is being achieved, Lean and Kanban propose the use of a specific metric called Cycle Time. It is clear that the challenge is to reach the shortest possible time for this indicator.

Following queuing theory, there are two aspects to be analyzed in order to measure the workflow efficiency. The first one is to measure the arrivals to each queue by how many units are arriving per time unit. The second aspect is to measure the length of service by the number of units processed per time unit. One way to counteract a significant ratio of arrivals is by grouping a small group of requests to be quickly delivered. Therefore the input or arrival queue fails to accumulate too many requests. If this is not done, then the processing may take a long time (if lots are large) and the queues or lines will get longer.

The other aspect to control is the length of service. If we look at our software development case, it shall be the activities inherent to the development. To accelerate the development cycle, the time spent on each process instance will be crucial. Any "processors" working at a lesser level of response than others will cause an increase on its queue and slowing down the development process. The cycle can be seen as a workflow where each stage of the product adds value to the product ordered (request) until it becomes a final product that adds value to the user (working software).

Work Frame

The framework proposed by Kanban has the following features:

- A board that allows visualizing the workflow in a clear and complete way.
- The work is divided into blocks, which like stages through which a request passes from beginning to its completeness.

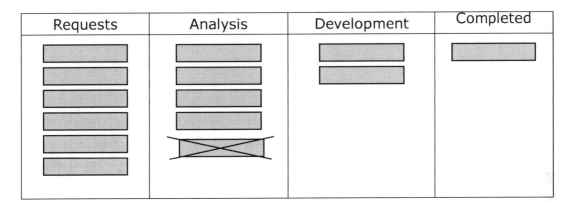

Requests	Analysis	Development	Completed

The use of this board tries to control two fundamental aspects of the process:

- Work in progress, which gets specific values assigned of how much work can be in progress in every stage during the development cycle. This restriction allows each workstation to focus on a finite and small number of concurrent activities. This will lead to work quickly with small lots, to reduce time wasted and to achieve shorter development cycles.
- The average time it takes the process to complete an element.

The Benefits of Kanban

What does Kanban add to the software development process?

- Displays all the workflow in progress.
- Identify the "bottlenecks" activities that are slowing manufacture of products and delaying the start of software production.
- Enable team's continuous learning by working in an integrated manner.
- Allow the team to manage their actions. The team members are the ones who pull the orders to advance into the workflow.

Pursued Axiom:

- Because we seek to deliver value quickly, we want to limit the amount of work to be done at all times.
- We want to finish the items before starting new ones.

It seeks to eliminate unnecessarily time items spent waiting. Examples:

- Certain functionality is requested and it is added to the list of requests to be developed. How much time passes that request on the list without being served?
- A request is analyzed. How long until it is assessed and allocated for its development?
- Once developed, is ready for testing. How long until it is tested?
- Errors are found. How much time passes before they are corrected?
- The product is ready. How long until it is place into production?

If we eliminate these times, we would be achieve:

- That the product ordered is in production and adding value to the customer faster.
- This way, we could pull another item and start its processing faster.
- We would be able to address and deliver many more requests in the same amount of time.

Why Kanban?

Kanban guidelines are followed to:

- Not build features that nobody needs at this time.
- Not write more specifications than those that can be coded.
- Not write more code than what can be tested.
- Not test more code than what will be delivered.

Costs Produced by Delays (Losses)

As previously discussed, one of the Kanban's pillars refers to reducing losses. However, how we interpret losses in software development process?

The aspects that produce developmental delays are:

- Rework: defects, errors, etc.
- Operating costs: planning, release generation, training, etc.
- Cost of coordination: timelines, resources, etc.

The use of Kanban intends to minimize these costs by:

- Working on small lots of timely requests which are rapidly developed and support potential changes throughout their entire working cycle. The introduction of these changes to the product may minimize associated costs. This process is designed in a way that the identification and implementation of changes is a transparent process with low impact on the product.
- When working on low-volume products "in process" the effort demanded by administrative tasks, planning and control is minimal. It needs to only focus on the control of two parameters: the cycle time and the maximum requests that can be processed per cycle status. The process to be followed is very simple, needs no major training and the creation of value is continuous. This results in a minimum impact on the working environment of the applicant.

Work Dynamic

The workflow is a continuous one as it is the production flow proposes.

Requests are coming to the list where they are prioritized. The team will "pull" from the list of requests those to be worked.

These requests will flow through the defined workflow. The team controls that the defined limits are not exceeded. If a limit is reached in any stage, the team cares about addressing bottlenecks over taking on new requests.

How are activities coordinated?

- First through a board that is visible to the whole team.
- Then, through quick monitoring meetings where a facilitator controls the following aspects :
  - Does the board represent reality?
  - Is there a request blocking work progress?
  - Are there any bottlenecks in any stage?
  - Is the process close to passing any defined limit?
- After the meeting, the indicators (response time and cycle) and the board are updated.

Indicators

The two most popular Kanban indicators are the average time of response (lead time) and the cycle time.

The time of response begins when the client makes a request and ends when it is delivered and ready for use. It is measured in time and not effort. Meanwhile, the cycle time starts when work begins on the request and ends when it is ready to be delivered.

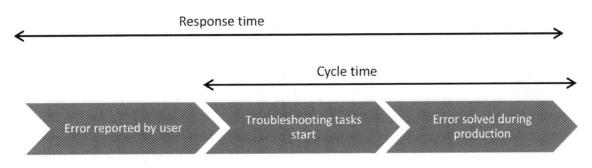

Another known aspect to control process performance is called throughput. This is the ratio of value deliveries made to the client during production. This indicator combines time of response and cycle. It indicates the number of functionalities that can be performed in a given time.

How to reduce time cycle?

Through the following:

- Reducing the number of requests that are "in process".
- Improving productivity or time of resolution across the different stages (processing time).
- Reducing rework.
- Getting adequate visibility of every aspect blocking the work.
- Getting each request to have a suitable size that can be managed in an agile way and adds value to the customer. This is known as the MMF or Minimal Markable Feature. These MMFs are split into stories, requests whose information is organized in cards (Kanban) and Tasks, in order to be administered through a board as seen above.

C.4 CONCLUSION ABOUT KANBAN

Kanban is one of the frameworks that follow the principles described in the agile manifesto.

Unlike other approaches, Kanban aligns more with the idea of continuous workflow where each request is separately prioritized and then developed. In contrast, e.g. Scrum, incorporates the concept of grouping lots by functionality and defines fixed time periods for delivery.

Kanban is an excellent framework to be incorporated in cases with any of the following characteristics:

- Each request requires quick response.
- Continuous processing is required, not only under defined time periods.
- The team has to be able to self-manage their work and to make decisions in order to speed timing and deliveries.
- Features and changes should be incorporated in later stages of the development cycle.

BIBLIOGRAPHY

BUTTRICK, Robert. (2010) Project Workout. Prentice Hall, New York.

COHN, Mike. (2004) User Stories Applied for Agile Software Development, Addison – Wesley, Boston

DAILEY, Kenneth. (2005) The Lean Manufacturing Pocket Handbook, Free Press, New York.

GEORGE, Michael M. (2005) The Lean six Sigma. Mc Graw Hill, New York.

GOODPASTURE John C. (2010) Project Management the Agile Way: Making It Work in the Enterprise. Ross Publishing, Florida

GONÇALVES Marcus (2010) Fundamentals of Agile Project Management: An Overview. Asme Press, New York.

HIGHSMITH James A. (2009) Agile Project Management: Creating Innovative Products. Adisson Wesley, New York

KNIBERG Henrik (2010) Kanban and Scrum - making the most of both. InfoQ, USA

LIKER, Jeffrey. (2004) The Toyota Way: 14 Management Principles From The World's Greatest Manufacturer. Free Press, New York.

MANTEL, Meredith. (2006) Project Management: A managerial approach. John Wiley & Sons, New Yersey.

MASCITELLI, Ronald. (2011) Mastering Lean Product Development: A Practical, Event-Driven Process for Maximizing Speed, Profits, and Quality.

MASCITELLI, Ronald. (2006) The Lean Product Development Guidebook: Everything Your Design Team Needs to Improve Efficiency and Slash Time to Market. Technology Perspectives. Technology Perspectives, California.

MASCITELLI, Ronald. (2002) Building a Project-Driven Enterprise: How to Slash Waste and Boost Profits through Lean Project Management. Technology Perspectives, California.

PRITCHARD, Carl. (2010) Risk Management: Concepts and Guidance 4th edition. ESI International, Virginia.

Project Management Body of Knowledge (PMBOK Guide). (2013) Project Management Institute, Pensilvania.

PURI, C. P. (2009) Agile Management: Feature Driven Development, Global India Publications, Nueva Delhi.

WOMACK, James P.; JONES, Daniel T.; ROOS, Daniel. (2010) Lean Thinking: Banish Waste and Create Wealth in Your Corporation, Revised and Updated. Free Press, New York.

WOMACK, James P.; JONES, Daniel T.; ROOS, Daniel. (2007) The Machine That Changed the World : The Story of Lean Production. MIT Press.

WOMACK, James P.; JONES, Daniel T. (2005), Lean Solutions : How Companies and Customers Can Create Value and Wealth Together. Free Press, New York.

SCHWABER Ken (2004) Agile Project Management with Scrum. Microsoft Press, Washington

LEAN AND AGILE PROJECT MANAGEMENT

How to be more agile in our projects?

The lean and agile philosophies are terms that define modern technics to make our projects fast and efficient, without adding costs or reducing quality.

The five principles of the lean thinking have its origin during the 90s decade in a Japanese automotive industry. This approach helps to improve the efficiency in mass production projects by focusing in adding value to the client and removing waste from the project value flow.

Ten years later the Manifesto for Agile Software Development and its twelve agile principles got popular. These ideas propose not to be too strict with plans and processes. Context can change permanently and we need to be flexible with the client in order to quickly adapt to those changes, if we want to submit the deliverables we have been asked for.

From these two currents of thoughts, one that focuses on mass production and another that focuses on software projects, in this book we will develop ideas 100% practical to improve efficiency and timeliness of any type of project management. Also, some of the concepts in this book will allow us to become more agile leaders in our daily activities.

The author, **Paul Leido**, has written eight books on Project Management. Some of them have been published by major Publishing companies. The author states that the benefits of reading this book are:

- Understand the lean-agile philosophy in a very simple way.
- Learn lessons from more than 20 real cases.
- Gain knowledge through more than 10 practical exercises.
- Save time and money when compared with other books.
- Be a better Project Manager.

Paul Leido is a PMP®, Master of Science in Project Analysis (University of York), MBA in Project Management (Universidad Francisco de Vitoria), MBA in International Businesses (Universitat de Lleida) and an Economist (Cuyo University).

Mr. Leido has trained more than 15,000 executives from international enterprises around the world. He works as the Director of **MasConsulting** and is a PMI® volunteer.

"PMI" y "PMP" are registered trademarks of the Project Management Institute, Inc.

www.pablolledo.com